THE LIFE
COACH

hamlyn

THE LIFE COACH

Become the person you've always wanted to be

Pam Richardson

A Pyramid paperback

First published in Great Britain in 2004 by Hamlyn,
a division of Octopus Publishing Group Ltd
2–4 Heron Quays, London E14 4JP

Copyright © Octopus Publishing Group Ltd 2006

Text copyright © Pam Richardson 2004

This material was previously published as *Life Coach*

ISBN 0 600 61320 8
EAN 9780600613206

A CIP catalogue record for this book is available from the
British Library

Printed and bound in China

10 9 8 7 6 5 4 3 2 1

Contents

Introduction

Life is not a dress rehearsal it's the real thing

Take a moment to answer these questions:

- **How are you living your life?**
- **Are you living and enjoying every moment?**
- **Are you just going through the motions?**
- **Do you keep telling yourself that one day your life will *really* start?**

The important thing is to ask yourself how you *want* to live your life and to what extent that is actually happening right now. If the answer to the second part is 'not enough', then this is the book for you. Whatever your reasons for choosing this book, it will give you an opportunity to:

- **work out where you are in your life**
- **decide where you would rather be**
- **open up new ways of thinking**
- **learn to close the gap.**

What is life coaching?

There are many definitions of coaching already, and many more will probably emerge, but – put simply – life coaching is a powerful process that supports people in releasing their true potential and in making changes in their lives.

First, there are those changes that we would like to make but can never find the time nor the energy to do anything about. Then there is also the tremendous pace of change in the world around us, which is unlikely to slow down in the future. Coping with change at work, at home or in life generally can be a huge challenge, and this is where life coaching can help.

How life coaching works

The coaching process is a very effective collaboration between you and your coach. The relationship is *non-judgemental*, meaning that no one is standing in judgement over you, and *unconditional*, that is designed purely to support you and to encourage you to achieve.

Coaching takes place through conversation. The conversation, however, is different from normal, social conversation. It is dynamic, focused and designed to move you forward in your life. Coaching raises your awareness and encourages you to take control of and responsibility for your life. Consider this for a moment – *you are the sum total of all the decisions that you have ever made in your life to date*.

If that is a daunting thought, take heart. You would not be the very special and unique person that you are otherwise. One thing is certain – there is no one else in the world exactly like you. Even if you are a twin or a triplet, you have your own unique personality. Once you 'own' it all, and acknowledge yourself regardless of whether some of those decisions were good, bad or indifferent, then you can move on.

Coaching assists you to realize your true potential

Developing your inner coach

It is a wonderful experience to be coached and to feel the support and encouragement of another human being who believes in your ability to achieve. However, the act of being coached will also help you to understand the process so that you can learn to coach yourself through any changes that you may want to make, or that you may have to make because of external influences.

There is a Japanese mindfulness puzzle that says 'wherever you go there you are' (see John Kabit-Zinn, *Mindfulness Meditation in Everyday Life*, London: Hyperion, 1995). Learning to coach yourself means that, wherever you go, there you are with your own coach on tap because he or she permanently resides within you – this is your *inner coach*. What a great way to travel through life.

Coaching yourself

By working through this book, you will learn how to use your own inner coach to achieve your goals. Coaching yourself involves:

- **listening to your inner self**
- **asking yourself powerful questions**
- **gaining clarity about what really matters to you in life**
- **stopping procrastination**
- **planning and taking action**
- **keeping focused on plans and their timeframes until you succeed.**

how to use
this book

This book will show you how coaching can help you to live your ideal life, whatever that means for you, through connecting with your inner coach. The approach used does not advise, suggest or tell you what to do, but encourages you to help yourself. It works largely by inviting you to ask yourself the right questions, so that you can arrive at your own best solutions. The book is divided into four main parts:

1. **Clearing the ground**

2. **Laying the foundations**

3. **Building your ideal life**

4. **The finishing touches.**

These are designed to guide you through the basic principles of coaching and then help you to apply these principles to your own specific situation in order to succeed in making any desirable changes. A book cannot create your ideal life by itself – it needs your help. Each section therefore gives you the opportunity to discover more about how you communicate with yourself.

Be your own best friend

Reading a self-help book is one thing, but putting what you read into action requires a desire to do so. This desire is usually linked to levels of self-esteem or self-worth. No matter what age you are, can you honestly say that you are your own best friend? If not, then what needs to happen for you to start becoming a friend to yourself? It might be as simple as having a special mug that you really like, or sorting through your clothes to decide what you feel good in and what you can give away. Whatever you do for yourself, you can choose to do it with a little more care and attention. A true friend accepts you for who you are, and listens to you in an unconditional way, not judging you but loving you *because* of who you are. Are you always so tolerant of or patient with yourself?

Never give up

When we look to make changes, we do not necessarily succeed at our first attempt. Many people then give up, simply saying to themselves, 'Oh well, this is just how life is', or, worse still, 'I'm hopeless, I can't do this', 'I'm not good enough', or 'I wasn't meant to have this'. Whatever you decide you want to do or change, if you find that you do not succeed at first, do not be put off – keep going and stay positive.

You may then discover why the changes you feel you want to make are challenging for you initially. You may discover that the changes you thought you wanted to make are not so important after all, and others will emerge. You will also discover what may have been holding you back, and how to deal with this and move on.

What is the difference between a coach and a friend or family member?

A coach does not bring his or her own agenda to the conversation and is detached from the outcome. Friends and family can care about you to the extent that they do not want you to take risks or make changes that will affect them. A coach simply believes in your ability to achieve whatever it is that you want for your life. Learning to coach yourself teaches you to trust *yourself* when you want to make a change in your life.

Who is the expert on your life? You are!

How does coaching differ from counselling or therapy?

Coaching is not a type of counselling or therapy. These highly-skilled interventions deal not only with the current issues a client is facing but also with their past, where there can be unresolved issues that still affect the individual. As you work through this book, if you become aware that you would benefit from the support of a counsellor, contact your nearest registered counselling organization by looking through your local phone directory or via the internet.

The spectrum of coaching

This spectrum is a description of two different coaching approaches. The whole spectrum is a picture of a 'directive' approach to coaching, in which a mentor or a coach could proceed to advise you or even tell you what to do. This is a very valuable intervention in the right circumstances. In business or in religious communities, the wisdom of an older, more experienced individual can be of great value. However, in other circumstances, this type of intervention can limit the opportunity to explore your own creativity. In a changing world, it does not always serve to do things the way they have always been done.

The bottom part of the spectrum is the 'non-directive' approach embodied in this book. As its name implies, it is less involved with directing and more about listening to what is going on for you, and working with you as you create the goal and strategy that is right for you. This style of coaching offers opportunities for your own unique, creative ideas to emerge.

DIRECTIVE

telling

training

teaching

giving advice

solution seeking

creative thinking

gaining clarity

questioning

listening

NON-DIRECTIVE

identifying your
goals

It is important to identify your final goals right at the start, before you become preoccupied with learning how coaching can help you. There are several ways to identify your goals, as described below. What is important is that you find a method that works for you, and that you keep a clear picture of what your ideal life represents to you as you work through this book to bring it into reality. Hold onto this picture so that you can bring this image back into your mind any time you want to or when you need some encouragement.

Creative visualization

This can be a powerful tool to use when you want to get a clear picture about any goal that you want to achieve. It is important, however, to give this kind of exercise the respect that it deserves. If this is the first time you have ever tried creative visualization, then enjoy the opportunity to imagine your ideal life. If you are familiar with it, then you already know what environment suits you best to maximize the power of this technique. What is important is that you find a quiet time and place to do the exercise.

Once you are settled, begin by taking a couple of deep breaths to start to relax. Check your body out. How relaxed does it feel? If you don't know, then start at the top and gently tense and relax each part of your body until you reach your feet. This helps by showing you the difference between being deliberately tense and relaxed when you let go of the tension.

Give yourself plenty of time to get a crystal-clear picture of the future that you want to create for yourself. Bring all your senses into play.

Keeping a clear picture of your ideal future in your mind helps create the reality

Imagine yourself living your ideal life:

- Where are you?
- Who are you with?
- What do you see yourself doing?
- What can you hear around you?
- How are you feeling?
- If you are somewhere that engages your senses of smell and taste, what are you aware of?

Using words and pictures

Another way to get a clear idea of what you want to create for your life might be hearing yourself describe what you want. Nowadays there are magazines that cover just about every aspect of life, and these may provide you with inspiration.

If you are creative, you could cut out pictures and produce a collage of your ideal life, or choose to paint or draw what you want to bring to life for yourself. Working with pictures as well as words engages the creativity of the right side of your brain, and also gives you access to the immense power of your subconscious mind.

Write down your personal definition of success:

Finding fulfilment, freedom, quality time with loved ones and a sense of well-being are common phrases in personal definitions of success. Now you have started to think about how you want your life to be, you can begin to work on how to close the gap.

Clearing the ground

This first section will help you to:

- *understand self-talk and recognize your inner coach*
- *sharpen your listening skills*
- *begin to turn negatives into positives*
- *develop your questioning techniques*
- *deal with 'I don't know'*
- *deal with doubt and fear*
- *overcome obstacles*
- *eliminate disempowering words*
- *clear away limiting beliefs that have held you back before.*

This 'clearing of the ground' is the vital first step in rebuilding the 'house' that is your life.

understanding
self-talk

Learning to tune into the conversations that you have with yourself is essential when you are looking to make a change. What you believe and hence tell yourself is possible, can have a powerful impact on what you achieve. This is often referred to as self-talk. What is surprising is that not all self-talk is positive and constructive. A coach believes that there are no limits to what you can achieve.

Time for a change

Cleaning up your self-talk can have a wonderful effect on self-limiting beliefs. The knock-on effect of dealing with these beliefs is a boost to your self-esteem and confidence. The point to remember here is that you may have been talking to yourself in a certain way for a very long time. The weeds may be very high on this plot of land called *your life*. You may have become unaware of what it is you actually say to yourself or how you say it. Our minds are never silent, unless we use meditation to reduce down the thoughts that fly backwards and forwards.

If you decide that you want to change your self-talk, then remember that changing a habit can take time – so be patient. Acknowledge every step you take that is moving you in the right direction. The 'fly on the wall' exercise (see page 16) is a good starting point for getting to know the nature of your own self-talk in order to identify areas for improvement.

Exercise: **Fly on the wall**

This exercise involves spending a few minutes each day listening to the chatter that is going on inside your own head. It is the first step to finding your own inner coach. Analyse what you hear:

- **What types of conversations do you have with yourself?**
- **Are there any negative thoughts?**

If you could characterize, or give a name to, the thoughts that produce the words you hear, what would you call them? As an example, a random survey of a group of office workers who did this exercise brought out a wonderful array of characters, some of which are listed below. There may be some names you recognize.

UNHELPFUL CHARACTERS	CHAMPIONS
Miss Afraid	Miss 'I can handle this'
Mr 'I need to be right'	Mr 'It's OK to make mistakes'
Miss 'Nobody likes me'	Miss 'I like me'
Mr 'I don't know'	Mr 'It's OK to ask'
Mrs Neurotic	Mrs 'Take it one step at a time'
Mr 'I'm not good enough'	Mr 'I am more than enough'
Mr Victim	Mr 'I own my own life'
Mrs Martyr	Mrs 'I value myself'
Ms Whinger	Ms Successful
Miss Undecided	Miss 'I can make decisions'
Mrs 'I'm hopeless'	Mrs 'I can do this'
Mr Critic	Mr Performer
Mr Confused	Mr 'I am confident in asking for clarity'
Mrs Procrastinator	Mrs 'Do it now'

What other names suit your particular cast of characters?

recognizing
your inner coach

Having analysed your self-talk, how can you choose which thoughts you want to carry on listening to and which ones you are going to weed out? This is where your inner coach comes in. To recognize the thoughts that come from your inner coach, run through this simple checklist. When you are tuning into your thoughts, are they:

- **Positive**
- **Believing in you**
- **Non-judgemental**
- **Encouraging**
- **Supportive**
- **Unconditional**
- **Wanting the very best for you.**

These are the qualities a coach would employ when listening to you and supporting you in order to plan and achieve your goals. It may be that to recognize this inner voice you will need to use a process of elimination.

Separate out the characters

Isolate the characters in your head that may be far from supportive, even downright obstructive, and you will be left with the thoughts that are the champions who fuel your strengths. There is the part of you that *can* achieve, that *is* creative, that *is* an effective leader, that *is* a good parent. This is the place where your inner coach will be found.

Who is your inner coach?

Your inner coach is that part of you that doesn't just listen to your dreams but encourages and supports you to make them a reality. Your inner coach:

- listens to your dreams
- believes in your ability to achieve, and says 'you can do this'
- uses questions to help you to assess your current position honestly and constructively – 'where are you starting from?', 'what have you done so far?'
- looks at all your options creatively with you – 'how many different ways can you think of to achieve your goal?'
- invites you to choose the option that excites you most – 'which idea do you like best?'
- helps you to plan your course of action meticulously – 'what are you actually going to do, and when are you going to do it?'
- checks your progress – 'how far have you got now?'
- challenges you to keep focused and on track – 'if you keep putting this off, how will that help you to achieve your goal?'
- acknowledges every achievement along the way – 'well done for doing that'
- celebrates your success with you – 'you're a star'.

YOU CAN DO THIS!

By now you may have reached the conclusion that listening is a very important part of coaching, so this is the next important topic.

Your inner coach listens to your dreams and helps you make them a reality

the power of
listening

When we engage in conversation socially, we tend to listen for information that we can relate to, and as soon as a gap appears we add our own experiences to join in the dialogue. If you can hear, this does not necessarily mean that you are also listening. Even if you are listening, you may not always hear what is being said in the way that it was meant. Effective communication is a wonderful thing, but it is not always that easy to achieve. Learning to listen actively can produce an immediate return on the investment of effort. This applies to actively listening not just to yourself but also to others. When a person is truly listened to, they grow in confidence and ability.

There are several different types of listening, as described below.

Listening to yourself

The ability to really listen to yourself is extremely important. It will help you discover what really matters to you in life and whether or not you are living your life in a way that honours this. Coaching helps you to separate out your listening skills depending on the circumstances that you find yourself in. Consider these questions:

- **What does it feel like to be truly listened to?**

- **What does listening to someone else really involve?**

- **How often do you find the time to listen to yourself?**

If your answer to the last question was 'not very often', then ask yourself what you can do to change this. What one small step can you take to make a difference? How can you identify the listening that goes beyond social listening and the kind of listening that is going to help you to listen more effectively to yourself?

Non-listening

Have you ever found yourself talking to someone and feeling that they are just not listening to you? How can you tell? Maybe it is the fact that their eyes keep wandering around the room to see who else is there, or their eyes glaze over, indicating that they are miles away.

If someone is exposed to non-listening regularly, it can have a negative impact on his or her self-esteem. This is particularly true for children. The message that is being sent out is that they do not have anything to say of value that is worth listening to. This can be translated into 'I have no value'.

Conversational listening

Here you are concentrating purely on the words being spoken. You are thinking 'What does this mean to *me*?' and 'How does this affect *me*?'. This type of listening is therefore sometimes referred to as *me too* listening. There are many occasions when this is totally appropriate:

- **chatting with friends over a drink where rapport is built by the sharing of experiences or moods**

- **in a job interview**

- **when you are being given instructions**

- **when you are being asked your opinion or advice on something.**

When you are listening to yourself, listening just to the words can be very helpful in identifying which character has centre stage at that moment. You can then decide whether you are going to continue to listen to them or to switch off the microphone.

On the other hand, if you are using this type of listening with someone who is trying to share his or her experiences with you, and all you are keen to do is to hear yourself talking, then this is not a particularly helpful level of listening to be using. Active listening (see page 21) is more appropriate in this situation.

Active or focused listening

The focus is on the speaker. You have removed yourself and your inner companions, which include your opinions and your experience, for the moment and you concentrate on the speaker. Here the listener is listening not just for the words that are spoken but also for the information that can be picked up from the speaker's expressions, emotions, tone, pace and intonation of the voice.

Active or focused listening helps you to gain clarity about the complete message that is coming from the speaker. You notice what they say, but also what they do not say. If someone has come to you for your support in achieving a certain goal that is important to them, then using this level of listening to analyse their situation is a true gift.

You listen for their values, their vision and what really inspires them. You can act like a mirror reflecting back what you hear, so that the speaker can really hear himself or herself thinking through what they want to do. Effective coaching uses active or focused listening.

Listening actively to yourself can help you discover what you really want in your life. By listening to the tone of your voice, you can identify whether an unhelpful inner character has crept on stage again.

Often we make assumptions that have little or no foundation. When you invite someone to share how he or she is feeling, then deeper understanding develops. The discipline here is not to interrupt. As children, we learn to say what we need to say in under 60 seconds on average. Why is this? We soon learn that we are going to be interrupted, so 'say it quickly or you might not get a chance to say it at all' becomes the motto.

Nancy Kline, in her book *Time to Think*, raises awareness of this by saying that when the talking stops the thinking does not. When someone knows that you are truly listening to them and that you do not intend to interrupt them, a wealth of creative thinking can take place. This applies just as much to listening to yourself as to listening to others.

Listening actively to yourself can help you discover what you really want in your life

Intuitive listening

 This takes listening into another dimension. Not only are you listening, with all of your senses, to the messages that you are receiving, but you are also tuned into your intuition. Intuition is slowly regaining its place in human communication after a couple of centuries of scientific dominance, where to some extent the view was that if you could not measure something then it did not exist. People are increasingly beginning to trust their intuition again. Going with your gut instinct can be very valuable when you are looking to make decisions about what you really want in life.

Really effective coaching uses both active and intuitive listening

How listening helps when making changes

When coaching yourself to make changes in your life, it is important to consider the impact this may have on others. Knowing how to listen and respond to other people who may be affected by your changes can be invaluable. Effective listening builds trust from the outset.

Mutual respect is very important here. Asking to be listened to is vital. Important relationships are underpinned by an understanding of the value of giving each other time and space to share dreams and ambitions. When a person has the time to express what they want, confident that they are being listened to and that they will not be interrupted or judged, then dreams can become reality. Inviting people to listen to you to understand the changes you want to make helps to gain the support of those close to you.

However, gaining external support is a bonus. The support that you can give yourself with the help of your inner coach is an essential part of accessing the strength, determination and confidence to live your life the way that you want. Learning to deal with the group of unhelpful characters that live inside your head, and who may look to hold you back, is the job of your inner coach.

turning negative
into positive

Case study: **Susan**

Susan was single and in her mid-20s. She had a good job but was constantly short of money, and this was really beginning to annoy her. She had always overspent by the end of each month, meaning that she had to pay extra bank charges as well. Susan had read about coaching and she was interested in how it could help people make changes in their lives. She decided to have a go at coaching herself with regard to her finances.

Firstly, and most importantly, Susan realized that she had had enough of her current situation. To benefit from coaching, you need to reach the decision that you are ready and willing to make a change. Susan asked herself how she wanted her financial position to change. She decided that she wanted to:

- **keep better track of her spending**

- **have some money left over at the end of the month**

- **use this money to start investing in a pension.**

Next, she asked herself 'what is it specifically that frustrates me about how I deal with my money?'. As she was going through the facts about her constant overspending and empty purse, she was stunned to hear a voice in her head saying 'you're hopeless with money'. It was a significant moment, just like someone turning on a light.

She knew that there was a certain amount of evidence that could support this statement. She chose not to blame and shame herself for once. She understood from what she had read about coaching that becoming aware of a negative belief provides a great opportunity to change that belief into something more positive and supportive.

Now that Susan had an awareness of what she believed about herself and money, she decided to work on a more positive belief. Then she could begin to look for positive evidence that this was true, to reinforce it. Susan decided to start telling herself 'I can manage my money'. She committed to looking for the positive evidence about her ability to manage money. She asked herself what one simple step she could take towards starting to manage her money. The idea that appealed to her most was to speak to her bank.

The following Saturday, she was sitting in her local bank getting lots of helpful ideas about budgeting, pensions and an agreed loan limit to support her in the short term. Susan now feels so much more confident about her financial position. She has also noticed that this confidence has spilled over into other areas of her life, as she feels more in control of how she is choosing to live.

Take a positive step

When you did the 'fly on the wall' exercise on page 16, you may have identified a few thoughts that are less than supportive of you, and that you would like to convert into something more positive. Choose one particular thought and reflect on it for a moment. You might even write it down. Now ask yourself how it helps you to hear yourself saying this. The rather obvious answer is that it doesn't. Think about how you could change this internal voice. What could you choose to say that is more positive and supportive?

Alternatively, think about a goal that you say you want to achieve but about which you never do anything. Ask yourself what is holding you back. Then have a go at applying active and intuitive listening to the answers that come up. What thoughts can you identify? Is there an inner cynic saying 'you'll never do that'? or inner sceptic saying 'what's the point?'? What are you choosing to listen to?

Remember you are your own best friend. If this is still one step too far, then imagine you are supporting your best friend to achieve a goal. What can you hear yourself saying to them? Whatever you decide to replace the original words in your head with, you need to be able to believe it. There is no point in starting to say something such as 'I am fantastic at everything I do' if you find another voice in your head saying 'since when?'. It is better to start off with something that can ring true for you such as 'I am good at what I do, and every day I am getting better'. Don't forget that your inner coach is that non-judgemental voice which believes in you unconditionally.

The power of affirmations

Affirmations are positive statements in the present tense relating to what you want to achieve. One simple but highly effective affirmation that can be applied to many situations is 'I can do this'. By continually repeating this to yourself, you can influence your subconscious mind and begin to alter limiting beliefs that may have held you back in the past. Positive affirmations can support you to bring about changes in your life.

Some people repeat a positive affirmation 50 times every morning and evening. Find out what works for you. However, remember to follow this up with *action* as well. Just telling yourself that you weigh 60kg (130lb) when you weigh 80kg (175lb) will not help to shift the weight if you are still consuming a lot more food than you actually need each day, and doing no exercise, whereas believing that you can be 60kg (130lb) and taking one step at a time consistently towards that goal can work wonders.

Looking for positive evidence

Once you have decided upon a positive statement that you can connect with, look out for positive evidence that supports this statement. If at first it isn't easy to find, that could be because you are just not used to looking for what *is* working in your life. You may have got used to seeing only what *isn't* working. Persevere, because like any habit it may take a while to change. The discipline is not to give in and fall back into the habit of looking and listening only for the negatives.

Give your inner coach permission to interrupt you and remind you of the question 'how does it help you to think like this?'. If you compiled your own list of inner characters, decide which champion you need to activate that can outweigh each unhelpful character. Coach yourself to turn the volume up on all your positive thoughts while turning the volume down on all the negative thoughts. Then consider in what other ways you can have fun while making your negative thoughts permanently redundant.

Exercise: **The one-day challenge**

For one day (24 hours), decide not to moan, whinge or say anything negative. If you catch yourself doing any of these, then start again from the beginning. It sounds easy, but it isn't. Once you have mastered one day, then go for two, three and so on, until you have made positive thinking and speaking a new habit and discovered your inner coach along the way.

Taking a step-by-step approach

Your inner coach can help bring clarity to your goals, and help you to break them down by supporting you to plan and take actions one small step at a time. If you have ever set yourself a huge goal, you will know that in reality you could not see yourself achieving it because you did not know where to start. What can happen then is that you actually don't start for fear that you will fail.

For example, even if you don't feel fulfilled or happy in your job, you may still carry on with it because you have bills to pay and maybe a family to support. The idea of making a change is just a distant dream. You carry on year in, year out, doing the same thing, going through the motions of life, but not really living it to the full. It is time to change all that. You *can* take yourself from where you are now to where you want to be.

Every project begins with a first step, and you have already taken the first one by sharpening your listening skills. You may even be listening to yourself and others now in ways that are new or different from what you have been doing to date.

You are your own best friend

the power of
questions

Non-directive coaching is about asking questions to support you to discover what is best for you by encouraging you to seek your own answers. This book can offer you questions that will help get you started and begin to raise your awareness and assist you in discovering what you want to do while your own inner coach 'limbers up'. As soon as your inner coach starts to come up with questions as well, then use your own instincts or intuition to decide which question is best for you. Yes, you can talk to yourself and not be crazy. Of course, if it is out loud and in public, then you might get one or two funny looks.

The role of this book is to show you how simple coaching is, yet how profound an effect it can have. A question might simply be offered to you that you had not thought of asking yourself, but always remember that the answers lie within you. Remember, if other questions pop into your head, you choose which ones are the most appropriate for you. Only you know the answer to that.

What are questions anyway?

Questions are invitations. They are invitations to share information or an opinion. In this case, the sharing is with yourself. Learning to coach yourself means learning to ask yourself effective questions that will help you to move on in your life. What helps here is a degree of natural curiosity.

Good communication is invaluable

How naturally curious are you?

Do you ever stop and reflect on what you do? What are the reasons behind doing the things that you do in the way that you do them? Is it because that is how you have always done things or how your family did things? In the world today, we may need to look at doing things differently for the very first time.

There is a bonus when you use questions effectively to decide what you want and how you want to achieve it. You can use this skill to communicate more effectively in all your relationships. Active listening and effective questioning are two skills that will always serve you well.

Learning to ask yourself questions

This is one of the most powerful ways of taking control of what you want to achieve in your life. Knowing that the answers lie within you and that you have the means of seeking them out can strengthen your self-esteem and build your confidence. This does not mean that you literally have all the answers, as in facts and figures. A coach does not assume that you have encyclopaedic knowledge, but believes that you can seek out what you need to know to help you to achieve your goals.

In the 21st century, we find ourselves in a 'knowledge revolution' where, in some sectors, it is extremely hard to keep up with all the latest research and new techniques. How are people supposed to cope? One way is to have the confidence to ask a question. Have you ever sat in a meeting at work and struggled to understand what was being talked about? If the language used is full of jargon or acronyms (such as 'jpg', 'pdf', 'CPD'), it can be even worse. I have listened to whole conversations that hardly had one recognizable word in them. What I have also seen is that, if one person is brave enough to ask the question 'what are we talking about here?', a sigh of relief often goes quietly round the entire room.

Types of question

There are several different types of question, as described below, and you need to know when you might choose to use each of them in communication generally, as well as which questions your inner coach would find useful to ask you. To begin with, the type of question you ask, and the way in which you ask it, can either open up a conversation or close it down.

Open and closed questions

One of the best ways to encourage a conversation is through the use of *open* questions as opposed to *closed* questions. Closed questions require only the answer 'yes' or 'no'. They are very efficient for confirming details or gaining commitment, but more detailed information is not usually forthcoming. Open questions have the benefit of helping to gather more information, as they create the opportunity for you to express fully what you wish to say.

Here are two closed questions:

- **Do you want to go out for a drink?**
- **Will you be at the meeting on Friday?**

The answer in both cases could be either yes or no. When you are coaching yourself, closed questions such as 'are you going to the gym today?' can help to prompt actions.

Here are two open questions:

- **Where would you like to go for a drink?**

(The question indicates that you have a choice and invites you to make that choice.)

- **What does work–life balance mean to you?**

(This question invites you to explore what matters to you in life.)

Open questions can help to develop motivation for what you are planning to do. For example, the question 'what are the benefits of going to the gym today?' presupposes that there are *benefits* to going to the gym, which can be very supportive of you and the way you feel about a goal that you have set yourself. The question also presupposes that you *are* going to the gym today.

Questions that presuppose

Coaching encourages you to become very specific about what you are going to do and, more importantly, when you are going to do it. So questions that tie you down positively are very important. Questions that have an element in them that indicates that you have already made the decision to do something can be very useful. For example, 'when will you tidy your bedroom?' takes it as read that you are going to tidy your bedroom, and it is just a matter of when. Try it out on a teenager if you have one! Which tone of voice would you choose to use in order to be non-confrontational?

Case study: **Janet**

Janet is becoming stressed over arrangements for Christmas. They always spend Christmas with her parents. However, this year her partner has suggested that they go and soak up some winter sun. She would love to, but she doesn't want to book anything until she tells her parents. She puts off phoning her mum because she doesn't know what to say and is concerned about upsetting her. Janet's inner coach simply asks 'when are you planning to make that phone call?'.

This simple question asks for a commitment and can halt evasion. Presupposing that she is going to make the call in the first place is a very powerful way for Janet to support herself to make it, as she is effectively saying that she believes that she is going to do it – it is just a case of when. All that remains is for Janet to work out what she is going to say. However, Janet would benefit from understanding that not all questions are helpful.

Leading questions

When a 'leading' question is asked, there is an implication that there is a right answer and that it is the answer that the questioner wants to hear. Leading questions stop people from thinking for themselves. These tend to be avoided in coaching. 'Your mother is going to be really upset, isn't she?' Which inner character would ask Janet in our case study this type of question? Could it be an inner control freak? It certainly doesn't sound like an inner coach.

Reflective questions

Leading questions can easily be turned into reflective questions by an inner coach, and this can make all the difference. An example of a reflective question is 'what is the best way to tell your mum that you are not coming for Christmas this year?'. Alternatively, it might be 'what do you hear yourself saying to your mum?'. Often we do not take action because we have a belief that limits us.

In our case study, it could be that Janet cannot see herself saying what she wants to say *without* upsetting her mum. Since upsetting her mum is not what she wants to do, she does nothing. However, it is Janet who then has to keep on coping with a situation rather than dealing with it.

Questions that bypass limiting beliefs

Powerful questions help you to break through limiting beliefs. Janet's inner coach asks her 'if you knew that whatever you were to say shows how much you love your mum, what do you hear yourself saying to her?'. This question contains a presupposition and it comes in two parts. The first part helps to bypass a limiting belief about not being able to share how Janet truly feels with her mum for fear of misunderstanding or of upsetting her, and the second part encourages creative thought.

Case study: **Janet's solution**

Janet realized, when she was thinking the whole thing through, that she saw her parents only three times a year, Christmas being one of them. She asked herself what options there were that would suit everyone, and then called her mother the following Sunday morning. This time, after their usual catching-up on news, she started by saying how much she was looking forward to seeing them both again. It was already October, the year was flying by and it would soon be Christmas. Janet had decided to share with her mother how she felt about visiting over Christmas, but, in order to work out how best to put it, she had decided to ask her mother the question 'What does Christmas mean to you?'.

She was stunned by what her mother shared with her. She really loved to have everyone home, but she wished that they could find a different way to celebrate. Christmas meant lots of cooking and she was finding that it wore her out these days. However, she did not want to disappoint anyone. Janet shared her idea about going away over Christmas for a change and her mother thought that was a great idea. They decided that Janet would visit the week before Christmas so she could see relatives and exchange presents. They would go out for a meal to celebrate her visit. Janet's mother also decided to talk with the rest of the family. By asking everyone in future what they wanted to do, she felt sure that they could *all* enjoy Christmas more.

If this is a situation that you can relate to, ask yourself what needs to happen for you to resolve it, and what type of conversation you need to have.

dealing
with 'I don't know'

What happens if you meet the 'I don't know' character when you ask yourself important questions? Where does this character come from and what can his or her role be in your life? You can't risk getting anything wrong if you say you don't know in the first place. Making a mistake, for some people, is a situation they will try to avoid at all costs.

How do babies learn to walk? Do they study a manual or go on a course? No. They just struggle up on their feet, take a first shaky step and fall down. Fortunately, they know nothing about failing or making mistakes, otherwise none of us would be walking around now. Their method of learning is very much trial and error – and determination. In fact, try stopping them from wanting to copy what they see everyone else doing and you will have a problem on your hands. Their attitude is 'if they can do it, so can I'.

Develop a 'have-a-go' attitude

It is quite a challenge to hang on to that wonderful have-a-go attitude to learning as we grow up. Why is that? We all enjoy the praise of our parents and teachers, and wanting to get things right in order to gain this praise is natural. However, getting things wrong or making a mistake can achieve the opposite. Peer-group pressure comes in here, too. Being ridiculed for making a mistake can be a painful experience that has a lengthy after-effect. No wonder we do our best to avoid making any mistakes. However, as an approach to making changes and moving forward in your life, this isn't particularly helpful.

Permit yourself to make mistakes

Giving yourself permission to make mistakes is very freeing. You can decide to silence the negative inner voices. If they have had it all their own way for some years, with comments such as 'you can't do that' or 'you'll only mess it up', then it's time to send them packing. After a certain age, the only voice that is being so critical is your own. There comes a point when we can choose to parent or teach ourselves – the past is history, and now is what matters.

Start listening to your inner coach. This voice will simply say 'you can do this' or 'you won't know unless you have a go'. Your inner coach can ask you 'what can you learn from this?' and 'how would you approach that next time?'. If you decide that you can learn from your mistakes instead of giving yourself a hard time, then you can really move on.

Confronting your 'I don't know' voice

If your 'I don't know' voice is persistent and loud, this is where your inner coach can be gently confronting – but not confrontational. Your inner coach is there to support and encourage you, not to stand in judgement of you. A few questions come to mind here, such as 'if you *did* know, then what would you say?'. This question, although remarkably simple, *always* gets a response. If you ask it of someone who, a moment earlier, was saying to you 'I don't know', and you remain silent no matter how long it takes, you can encourage that person to engage with their thought processes and they *will* come up with an idea.

When coaching yourself, you can get away with all sorts of questions – such as 'if *you* don't know what is best for you, who does?' or 'what needs to happen for you to know?'. The rewards of taking control of making decisions are high self-esteem and a self-assurance that can carry you through any situation.

Coaching yourself can be a lot of fun

dealing
with doubt

How can you use coaching questions to help you to deal with doubt? First, coaching helps you to gain clarity. Use your questioning skills to identify any emotions that could hold you back from making positive changes in your life:

- **What is going on for me here?**
- **Who am I being right now?**

Once you have identified what you are dealing with, you can work with your inner coach to decide what you are going to do. Coaching is all about taking action in order to move forward. You can deal with doubt by:

- **listening to your self-talk and keeping it positive**
- **planning to take one small step at a time**
- **acknowledging yourself each step of the way.**

Believe in yourself

How often do you hear yourself using words such as 'try' or 'hopefully'? These words, and words like them, do little to encourage and support you to believe that you can do things. They have embedded doubt in them. When you are looking to make changes, these little words can have a powerful impact on how you approach a task.

For example, have you ever *tried* to clean your teeth? Or do you just decide to do it? The word 'try' actually brings doubt into your mind. What might happen if you 'try' to clean your teeth?

'Hopefully, we'll win the game.' This way of talking again brings doubt in and does not convey as much belief and conviction as 'we *can* win this game'.

Using a step-by-step approach

When coaching someone to achieve a goal, a coach often asks 'what is the first thing you can do that will take you one step towards your goal?'. This encourages you to break down a goal into manageable steps, helping you to succeed and to see results quickly. You can also adjust your path, whenever necessary, to keep yourself on track.

Success breeds confidence

Doubt disappears, to be replaced by confidence, after you have gained the evidence of a few successes, however small they might be. When there is an element of doubt in your mind, always go with how you *feel*.

Trust your intuition

dealing
with fear

Fear comes in all sorts of guises, but fear of failure or rejection and fear of success are quite common.

Fear of failure or rejection

There are many ways to limit yourself and the fear of failure can stop you from attempting something new or different. How you talk to yourself has a powerful influence:

The really negative inner characters can have a field day:

- **'You can't do that.'**
- **'You will only make a fool of yourself, again.'**
- **'Don't be stupid.'**
- **'They'll laugh at you.'**
- **'What now?'**

The fearful characters play the game of 'what if':

- **'What if it goes wrong?'**
- **'What if it doesn't work?'**
- **'What if you mess it up?'**

Imagine that you want to apply for promotion, but your new job would involve you making presentations. You are petrified of having to stand up and talk in front of people. All you can hear in your head is:

- **'You're hopeless at public speaking.'**
- **'What if I dry up?'**
- **'What if I can't answer a question?'**
- **'What if they start to laugh at me?'**

So you begin to talk yourself out of applying for the job, ably supported by Miss 'You're Hopeless' or Mr Fear of Failing. After listening for a while, your inner coach asks a couple of questions:

- **'What's going on here?'**
- **'How is it serving you to listen to this?'**

Now you have a choice. You can carry on listening to negative self-talk that will continue to hold you back in your life, or you can start to work on how you want to develop new skills and move forward. What's it going to be?

Fear of success

Fear of succeeding can be just as daunting. Apart from your inner cynic that can produce gems such as 'that was a fluke' or 'you won't do that again' at the drop of a hat, there are all sorts of fearful questions that can come up here:

- **'What will people expect of me?'**
- **'What responsibilities will I have now?'**
- **'What will people think of me now?'**
- **'Can I keep this up?'**

Your inner coach can help you in this situation by listening out for:

- **positive self-talk**
- **what is working (not what isn't)**
- **how you can succeed (not how you can fail).**

So, when you hear 'what if' followed by doubt, your inner coach can support you to adopt a more positive approach. For example, it might replace 'what if I dry up?' with 'what can I do to ensure that I do not dry up?'. You can raise your own awareness that good preparation and plenty of rehearsal can overcome these fears. You could substitute 'what if I can't answer a question?' with 'what can I say that maintains my authority?'. Coach yourself to take control by realizing that nobody expects you to have all the answers all the time. It is far better to be honest and to say you do not have the answer than to try to bluff your way through and appear flustered. Being honest, finding out and getting back to them promptly is what impresses people.

Overcoming failure and success

Your inner coach can also turn the whole situation on its head by asking 'what if you can do it?' or 'do you remember a time when you did that?'. Some people have got so used to turning up the volume on their 'can't do' character that their 'can do' voice is never heard. Ask yourself:

- **Can I cope with failing? Once you can say yes, then you are free to have a go.**
- **Can I cope with succeeding? Once you can say yes, then you are free to grow.**

Here is another question: 'If you knew you could succeed, what would you be doing?' In your answer, be really descriptive:

- **What do you see yourself doing that brings you success?**
- **What do you hear people around you saying to help you to succeed?**
- **What feelings do you have when you have succeeded?**

Case study: **Graham**

Graham had tried to give up smoking several times before. Each time he had lasted a couple of weeks and then his willpower had caved in, usually when he was out with his mates. They would keep offering him a cigarette, and in the end he would give in. Now he had got to the stage where he was afraid to fail again. Each time he had given in before, his inner voice had said things like 'you're pathetic' and 'you can't stick at anything, can you?'.

One day Graham picked up a book on coaching, and a new world opened up. He began to see that he was sometimes not aware of what was holding him back. He decided to listen to his self-talk objectively for the first time. He also went in search of a voice in his head that said 'you can do this'. The first thing he heard was 'I ought to give up smoking'. With the help of his inner coach, he started to challenge some of the statements that he heard.

Inner coach

That statement 'I *ought* to give up smoking' – who says?

Wherever the expectation was coming from, it was external.

Graham

'Well, I know it's bad for me, but that doesn't seem to be enough to *make* me stop.'

Graham had not yet decided to choose to give up smoking. Using the words 'make me stop' reinforced the idea that some external force was supposed to achieve this goal.

Inner coach

Graham

What do you want to be, Graham, a smoker or a non-smoker?

There was a long silence. Graham had never thought of it like that before.

'I really want to be a non-smoker.'

Once he became aware that he had a choice and, more importantly, aware of his power to choose, he decided to exercise this power, with stunning effect.

When you are a non-smoker, what do you see yourself doing?

I can afford to buy and run a car.

What does that mean to you?

I will be able to go over and see my girlfriend more easily. I will have more money, so will be able to get away at weekends for a break.

Sounds great. What's holding you back?

Graham remembered the negative statements that he listened to each time he failed.

When *have you* stuck at something?

I finished my degree, even though I found it difficult. At work, I finish reports and hit my deadlines every time.

That's impressive. Who are you in relation to smoking?

Inner coach

Great. What do you see yourself doing as a non-smoker?

Sounds good. What obstacles might get in the way of you being a non-smoker?

How do you see yourself overcoming this?

Graham

I am a non-smoker.

I am throwing my cigarettes away.

When I am out drinking, I usually have a cigarette. My mates all smoke. They'll give me a hard time.

It is my choice whether I am a smoker or not, not theirs. I am a non-smoker. I will focus on getting my car and having more money to spend the way I choose to now.

Graham decided to listen only to the voice of his inner coach, who encouraged him all the way. He ignored any negative voices that tried to throw him off track. His friends became very supportive when they realized he was serious. Graham has been a non-smoker for six months. He has a car that is his pride and joy, and his relationship with his girlfriend has grown. She is a non-smoker, so appreciates Graham for becoming a non-smoker too, and they can afford to go out more together. Graham is feeling really good about things because he has realized that, when he makes a conscious choice to do something, nothing stops him.

gaining
clarity

A coach uses a question starting with 'why' only with some caution. The reason for this is that it can lead to a situation where you feel you have to defend yourself or justify a particular position. For example, a question such as 'why didn't you do that?' may well keep you firmly stuck in the past, when what really needs to happen is for you to move forward.

You can start a much more productive conversation by asking 'what do you think is stopping you at the moment?'. Giving yourself an honest answer without judgement gives you the opportunity to deal with what is holding you back. It could be as simple as the fact that you are not working towards the goal that you want, so you are not really committed, hence the importance of gaining clarity about your goal when you are looking to make a change.

Vague goals, vaguely described, are neither easy to focus on nor to plan for. Taking the time to identify what you really want to achieve is always time well spent, so the more curious you can become the better.

Give yourself an honest answer without judgement

Practising for success

Initially, choose a goal that is not going to require too much of a change, so that you can get some practice at making a change. This might be choosing to:

- **do a simple stretching exercise when you get up, to start you off on the road to doing more exercise eventually**
- **decide what to wear for work the night before, so that you do not end up rushing so much in the morning**
- **drink more water and less coffee at work.**

Work through the following questions and stages until you attain your aim:

- **What are you choosing to do?**
- **What needs to happen for you to do this?**
- **If you want support to do this, who will you ask?**
- **What are you going to say to them?**
- **When are you going to talk to them?**
- **What obstacle, if any, can you see getting in the way?**
- **How will you overcome this?**

As you work through this book, you will discover more about what may hold you back from making changes, as well as lots of ideas to support you to make those changes.

The power of good communication

One of the aims of this book is to encourage you to increase the effectiveness with which you communicate with yourself. Coaching encourages you to remind yourself of the skills that you have; *remind* you, not teach you or give you skills – you already possess them.

The philosophy behind coaching is to honour and respect your natural ability and to offer you the opportunity to enrich it. You can fine-tune your listening and questioning ability to access an even deeper understanding of who you are choosing to be. This in turn assists you to communicate who you are more effectively to those around you.

the power of
words

The actual words and phrases you choose to describe where you are in your life can reveal a great deal to you about yourself and what you believe it is possible for you to achieve. This becomes crucial when these words are the ones you hear yourself using on a regular basis. Raising your awareness of the power of words can assist you to become really clear about:

- who you want to be
- what you want to do
- what you want to have in your life.

Simple changes to the three phrases above can make subtle but significant changes to their influence. Is the way you are living your life driven by:

- who you *think* you should be?
- what *someone else* wants you to do?
- what *social pressure* says you ought to have in your life in order to be considered successful?

If you are more likely to describe yourself in relation to outside influences, this will have an impact on how you live your life. Before you go any further ask yourself a question; 'What needs to change in order for me to take control?'.

Giving away personal power

Coaching works on the basis that you do have choices in life, and what you do with them is up to you. If you choose to rely on other people to make decisions for you, to tell you what to do, and to bully you to do things, how can you complain that your life isn't how *you* want it to be? You have relinquished your *personal power*. Consider these questions:

- **In what ways do you give away your personal power? And to whom?**
- **What do you gain by giving away your personal power?**
- **What do you lose by giving away your personal power?**

Giving away your personal power can make you feel as if you are not responsible for anything that happens, particularly when things go wrong. Instead, you can blame someone else. This is one way to survive, but it is an extremely limiting way to live. What can be lost is self-esteem and confidence – a high price to pay.

Small words, big impact

When asked 'how are you?', do you reply 'not so bad, thank you'? This means 'not so good either'. When you acknowledge yourself for doing something, is 'quite' hiding in the sentence ('I did quite well')? If someone tells you that you look *quite* nice, be aware of just how undermining that little word can be to your self-esteem and confidence.

Phrases such as 'I ought to do this' and 'I have got to do this' are often said without understanding what a powerful impact they have. By creating an external expectation on you, rather than an internal decision or choice to do something, you are allowing yourself to engage in a conversation with 'poor old me' whenever you want. However, you will need much more energy to fulfil a task from this position.

Not all activities in life can guarantee to be exciting or even interesting – they just need to be done. You can still control the way that you approach such a task. There can be a significant difference in how you feel about an activity depending on whether you feel you *must* do it as opposed to *choosing* to do it. Your inner coach can listen for this type of phraseology and invite you to change it to something more empowering. Choosing to add a spoonful of fun to even the dullest activity can work wonders.

Case study: **Mary**

Mary hated her weekends. She worked hard all week and then *had to* catch up with the chores at the weekend. It had got to the stage that she resented it so much that she lay in bed most of Saturday morning feeling depressed and lethargic. When she did eventually drag herself out of bed, she collapsed in front of the television in her dressing gown for most of the afternoon, watching anything that was on, and eating crisps and chocolate.

She convinced herself that chilling out like this was what she needed to do after working all week. By the evening, she felt even worse because her flat was a mess, she had a pile of dirty clothes and no food in the house. Sunday followed a similar pattern.

This is how coaching helped Mary.

Inner coach	Mary
What is it about weekends that you hate?	
	I have got to do all the chores.
... have 'got to'?	
	Well, the flat is a mess, I have got to do the washing and the washing-up, and there is usually no food in the house by Friday.
What would you choose to do at the weekends?	
	I would choose to have time to enjoy myself doing the things I want to do.
What sort of things do you enjoy doing?	
	I would like to meet up with some friends, go shopping, go for a drink or go to the cinema.
What is stopping you doing this?	

Mary started to talk about her weekends and how she felt she ought to be spending time on chores. She had got to the stage that she was just not doing them. However, because her flat was a mess and she had not done any washing, she now did not feel like going out either.

Inner coach	Mary
How would you like your flat to be?	
	I want it to be clean and tidy without me having to spend all my free time sorting it out.
What does 'clean and tidy' mean to you?	
	The bathroom and the kitchen cleaned. All my clothes put away in the bedroom and the living room clear of cups and plates, magazines and stuff. A bit of dusting and vacuum cleaning – nothing major, just enough for it to feel nice.
What other jobs need doing on a regular basis?	
	I need to do some food shopping and wash some clothes.

The coach summarized this list of tasks and repeated it to Mary, who agreed that this was what she needed to do each week to service herself and her flat.

When would you choose to do these jobs?

At this point, Mary began to realize not only that there was not so much to do after all, but also that she could definitely organize things so that she had time for herself at weekends as well. It just needed a slight adjustment in how she felt about it all and that was influenced by how she described it to herself.

Once Mary was clear in her own mind about what she could choose to do in order to have her weekends to enjoy herself as well, she even began to break down a few jobs to do during the week. Keeping her flat looking tidy eventually became a *pleasure* rather than a *chore*. She enjoyed buying flowers to decorate her home, and began to invite friends back for supper, which she had never done before.

Choose to control the way you approach your tasks

Shifting the emphasis

In the case study on pages 47–49, Mary's coach simply asked her to be a little more specific regarding what she hated about her weekends. Then the coach listened to what Mary said, picked up on the phrase 'have got to' and invited Mary to raise her awareness of what that phrase meant to her to gain more clarity. Focusing on positives rather than negatives, her coach asked Mary to explore what she would rather do, and this produced a list of enjoyable activities. Her coach was then able to challenge her by posing the question 'what is stopping you doing this?'. This invited Mary to take control, since Mary was answerable only to herself.

Mary's use of phrases such as 'ought to be spending time on chores' was not a very inspiring way to view what needed to be done in order for her to have a pleasant environment to live in *and* a thriving social life. By clarifying what actually needed doing, Mary also realized that this was not as onerous a task as she had thought. By focusing on how she wanted to spend her time once her flat was organized, she could plan how to achieve this with new energy. Choosing to take control was the way to achieve her ideal weekend. Learning to use this simple process of listening and questioning is how you can coach yourself to have your life exactly how you want it.

Taking control

Your coach is totally supportive of you, but that can mean challenging you to take control of your life and take action rather than just sitting there wishing it were different. A coach can be confronting, but is never confrontational. When you are coaching yourself, it is essential that you show yourself the same respect while at the same time not letting yourself off the hook.

'I OUGHT TO BE SPENDING TIME ON CHORES'

'I WILL CHOOSE TO SPEND ONE HOUR DOING CHORES ON SATURDAY'

Exercise: **Make choices**

Think of situations in which you hear yourself using the following phrases:

- I ought to ...
- I must ...
- I've got to ...
- I should ...

For example, you might find yourself saying things like:

- **I must visit my mother**
- **I've got to clean the car**
- **I should answer the phone whenever it rings**
- **I ought to fill out my tax form**
- **I ought to lose weight.**

Jot a few down, and then see what happens if you replace those phrases with 'I choose to' or 'I choose not to'. How does that feel? If you are choosing to do something, think about how you can make it as enjoyable as possible, or do it with good grace. If you choose not to do something, then decide to whom you need to delegate the task. This applies to a task like filling out your tax form, since simply choosing not to do it is not a solution. However, it does not always have to be you who actually performs the task.

Case study: **Peter**

Peter has been avoiding visiting his mother because she tends to talk negatively about everything and he finds it rather depressing. However, by not visiting her for weeks at a time, he also feels guilty. He loves his mother, and now she is on her own and doesn't get out much any more. She lives about an hour's drive away, so, by the time he has driven there, spent a couple of hours with her and driven back, most of his Sunday has gone.

First of all, Peter decides to use the phrase 'this coming Sunday I am choosing to visit my mother'. This is good, so far. He feels better that he has made the decision to visit her, as it has been two months since his last visit. Then he decides to work out how he can make his visit more enjoyable, not just for himself but also for his mother. The one thing that she does show an interest in is her houseplants. He checks out where her nearest garden centre is and decides that he will take her there.

Peter and his mother enjoyed the best day together that they could both remember for a long time. He stayed until quite late because he wanted to help her repot her plants, and he felt happy as he drove home because he could see how much his visit had meant to his mother. He decided to ring her once a week in future for a chat. He also made the choice to take her out one Sunday a month.

Peter felt a new confidence in himself. He realized that the way he had been dealing with the guilt that he felt when he did not visit his mother was to convince  himself that it was actually *her* fault because she seemed to be negative about everything. He now realized that he had the power to influence his own thinking and to deal with situations more positively.

Peter decided to transfer this way of being to other areas of his life as well.

Spice up dull tasks

Let your inner coach challenge you to work out how to make whatever needs doing more interesting. Whatever it is, you can find a way to make it more enjoyable. Listening to the radio or some music can transform a boring task. What other ideas can you come up with? Decide which one you will use next time you have something to do that needs energizing.

Global words

Think about the impact that words such as 'never' and 'always' – global words – can have on your confidence. When you were doing the visualization exercise on page 13, you may have heard a voice using these words in a negative way. By listening to you and feeding back these global words, your inner coach can help you to raise your awareness of reality compared to your *perceived* reality.

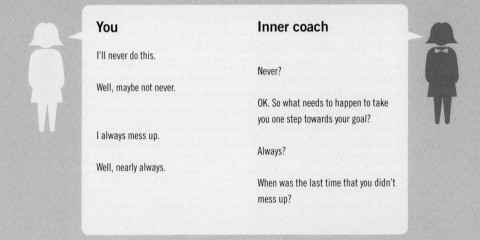

You

I'll never do this.

Well, maybe not never.

I always mess up.

Well, nearly always.

Inner coach

Never?

OK. So what needs to happen to take you one step towards your goal?

Always?

When was the last time that you didn't mess up?

Deciding to activate your inner coach can gently challenge you when you decide to 'go global' in a way that is not supportive of what you are looking to achieve.

dealing
with limiting beliefs

Take a moment to reflect on a time or situation when you found yourself using a global word negatively, and explore the impact of challenging this limiting belief. Simply look for an example of a time or situation when the evidence does not support your global statement. Notice how you feel as you start to dismantle this statement. Ask yourself the following questions:

- **How keen am I to locate an experience that *contradicts* a negative statement about myself, or do I sense any resistance? (You can often recognize resistance by a little voice that says 'yes, but ...'.)**
- **If there is resistance, what character is holding centre stage in my head right now?**
- **What benefit do I gain by listening to him or her?**
- **What benefit will I gain by refusing to listen to him or her?**
- **How do I want to deal with this character?**
- **What course of action will strengthen my self-belief and my confidence in myself to achieve?**

I CAN DO IT!

I CAN'T DO IT...

Negative statements about yourself, that you choose to listen to, do absolutely nothing to support you to achieve a fulfilling, purposeful life. Make no mistake, either – what you choose to believe about yourself *is* your choice. Whatever it takes, you *can* choose to change.

Origins of beliefs

Our original beliefs are developed during our childhood. A young child comes from a place where anything is possible, but as they grow up something happens to change this perception. Every child is a genius until someone convinces them that they are not.

Between the ages of one and 18 years, you are likely to hear many more negative statements than positive ones. In a word-association exercise with an average seven-year-old, when asked what words they associate with the word 'parent' many will immediately come up with 'no' or 'don't'. Alarming as that may sound to all of you who are caring, encouraging parents, it is interesting to examine what happens in order to get this result.

- **To keep a young child safe when they are running ahead of you on the pavement, if there is any chance that they could run into the road, what do you say? Perhaps it is 'don't run', or something similar.**

- **If they are in front of the fire and looking as if they might get too close, perhaps you might say 'no'.**

These words are quickly delivered and usually have the desired effect of stopping the child in question from hurting themselves. The alternative is to engage in a possibly lengthy, reasoned conversation as to the consequences – that if they carry on doing whatever it is they are doing they could end up getting hurt. By this time it could be too late. No wonder we hear the word 'no' so many times in our life.

However, the result is that we can carry this negativity into our adult life, and allow it to affect the way we think and limit what we believe we can achieve. This is why, of all the thousands of thoughts that we have on average each day, a large number can be negative. Many of our thoughts are repeated thoughts, and, therefore, serve only to reinforce the negative.

If you feel that now is a good time, you might like to have another go at the one-day challenge exercise on page 26.

Every child is a genius until they are convinced otherwise

Dealing with limiting beliefs

If you hold a negative or limiting belief about yourself, what can you do about it? The first step is recognizing it, because only then can you begin to change. Dr Anthony Grant, working in the Coaching Psychology Unit at the University of Sydney, has studied the psychology of change. He talks about:

- **taking the time to contemplate a change**
- **being ready to embark on a change**
- **change requiring preparation**
- **relapse being normal.**

If you take this into account, it can help to keep you on track if there are any changes that you decide you want to make in your life.

Exploring beliefs about yourself

Are you aware that you hold a limiting or negative belief about yourself? If so, can you put it into words? Think about what evidence you are aware of looking for to reinforce this belief – you may surprise yourself that there isn't any in reality. Consider what you could choose to say and believe about yourself that is more positive. You could even record this somewhere as a reminder. Then identify where you can look for the positive evidence that this new belief is true.

This is where coaching is so powerful, because when you coach yourself your inner coach is listening only for the brilliance in you. This can help you to reinforce a new belief as you work to establish it. Whatever the quality of parenting or schooling that you may have had in the past, there comes a time when you can choose to coach yourself to achieve. You can choose what you believe about yourself and what you say to yourself. Positive thoughts and self-acknowledgement are a powerful combination for lasting success in whatever you choose to do in life.

When you choose to raise your own awareness and to take responsibility, you empower yourself either to keep things as they are or to make changes. Recognizing the thoughts that have centre stage in your mind at any moment and being able to identify the character that is producing them, gives you the choice to engage with those thoughts or to dismiss them.

Relapse is normal

If you find that you are struggling to make and sustain a change at this early stage, then remember that relapse is normal, and keep reading and working with the ideas in this book. What you are doing right now is practising making changes before you start to lay the foundations on which you can build the life you really want that you created right at the beginning of the book.

When it comes to making changes, here are two useful mottos:

- **You won't know until you have a go.**

- **If at first you don't succeed, take stock and have another go.**

Achieving good balance

In the course of working with the material in this book, you have the opportunity to coach yourself, not only to influence the relationship that you have with yourself for the better, but also to impact positively on *all* your relationships. Nowadays, trying to balance all the different relationships and areas of life can become quite a juggling act. It is not always easy to achieve and maintain the balance, and that is where coaching can be so valuable. Taking a step back and adopting an objective view of your life right now helps you to remind yourself what areas are your priorities. This is important in maintaining a balance if you are contemplating making a change.

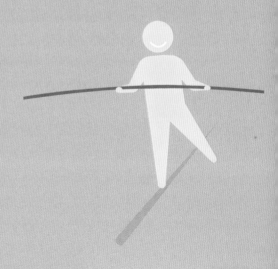

Exercise: **Find your wheel of life**

The eight sections in the wheel of life represent balance. Regard the centre of the wheel as representing 'very dissatisfied' and the outer edge as 'very satisfied'. Shade in the amount of each segment that represents your level of satisfaction with each sector of your life currently. Be instinctive here, as this often reveals more than if you were to have a logical, rational debate with yourself. You are looking for an impression of how you feel right now. Notice what shape you arrive at. Your wheel may not be round!

If you are still not sure what to do, have a look at the example bottom left.

PHYSICAL ENVIRONMENT

WORK/ CAREER

FUN AND LEISURE

MONEY

PERSONAL GROWTH

HEALTH/ FITNESS

RELATIONSHIPS

FAMILY

This exercise gives you a very graphic view of how satisfied or fulfilled you feel in different parts of your life at any one moment. What is important to focus on here is what fulfilment or satisfaction means to you. Fulfilment is a very personal thing that is also constantly evolving. What we find fulfilling when we are in our 20s may have changed by the time we reach 50. Take the time to decide which area is a priority for you right now. Working on one area at a time will produce better results than trying to change too much all in one go. Focusing on making changes in one area can, however, have a natural, positive knock-on effect on other areas anyway.

Relapse is normal

If you find that you are struggling to make and sustain a change at this early stage, then remember that relapse is normal, and keep reading and working with the ideas in this book. What you are doing right now is practising making changes before you start to lay the foundations on which you can build the life you really want that you created right at the beginning of the book.

When it comes to making changes, here are two useful mottos:

- **You won't know until you have a go.**

- **If at first you don't succeed, take stock and have another go.**

Achieving good balance

In the course of working with the material in this book, you have the opportunity to coach yourself, not only to influence the relationship that you have with yourself for the better, but also to impact positively on *all* your relationships. Nowadays, trying to balance all the different relationships and areas of life can become quite a juggling act. It is not always easy to achieve and maintain the balance, and that is where coaching can be so valuable. Taking a step back and adopting an objective view of your life right now helps you to remind yourself what areas are your priorities. This is important in maintaining a balance if you are contemplating making a change.

Laying the foundations

Becoming really clear about what you want in your life is essential before you set out to create this life. Without this understanding, it is difficult to plan specific actions and achieve your goals. There is also the possibility that you will end up compromising your goals and perhaps settling for second best. In the first part of this book, you were given the opportunity to:

- **check out how the land lies for making the changes that you want to make in order to realize your ideal life**
- **clear away a few limiting beliefs**
- **make some adjustments to your picture as you give yourself time to reflect on what really matters to you in life**
- **practise making small, sustainable changes so that you build up your confidence and succeed at making more life-changing choices later on.**

In this part of the book, you are moving on to:

- *establish where you are at the moment*
- *understand what is involved in change*
- *focus on the positives and the personal*
- *define and sort out your roles*
- *become assertive and find your voice*
- *bring TRUST to all your relationships*
- *discover the power of your core values*
- *work on your self-esteem*
- *create goals using the SMART model*

Identifying your starting point

B

A

Before you can work out how to get to point B, your goal, you need to know exactly where point A is, that is where you are right now. Then you can start to plan small, achievable steps to get you all the way from A to B. You can use the following two exercises to identify your starting point.

Exercise: **Find your wheel of life**

The eight sections in the wheel of life represent balance. Regard the centre of the wheel as representing 'very dissatisfied' and the outer edge as 'very satisfied'. Shade in the amount of each segment that represents your level of satisfaction with each sector of your life currently. Be instinctive here, as this often reveals more than if you were to have a logical, rational debate with yourself. You are looking for an impression of how you feel right now. Notice what shape you arrive at. Your wheel may not be round! If you are still not sure what to do, have a look at the example bottom left.

PHYSICAL ENVIRONMENT

WORK/ CAREER

FUN AND LEISURE

MONEY

PERSONAL GROWTH

HEALTH/ FITNESS

RELATIONSHIPS

FAMILY

This exercise gives you a very graphic view of how satisfied or fulfilled you feel in different parts of your life at any one moment. What is important to focus on here is what fulfilment or satisfaction means to you. Fulfilment is a very personal thing that is also constantly evolving. What we find fulfilling when we are in our 20s may have changed by the time we reach 50. Take the time to decide which area is a priority for you right now. Working on one area at a time will produce better results than trying to change too much all in one go. Focusing on making changes in one area can, however, have a natural, positive knock-on effect on other areas anyway.

Exercise: **Complete the pre-coaching questionnaire**

Having gained a visual overview of how your life feels at present, go on now to explore some thoughts in more depth. Write down the answers to the following questions as honestly and fully as you can.

- **What do you want to achieve through coaching?**
- **What is most important to you in life?**
- **Who is most important to you?**
- **What goals have you achieved so far in your life?**
- **What goals have you set aside as unachievable?**
- **What are your natural gifts/abilities?**
- **What aspects of your life/work do you enjoy most?**
- **What aspects of your life/work do you enjoy least?**
- **What do you feel that you are putting up with?**
- **What personal habit or trait would you like to change?**
- **In what areas of your life do you want to move forward?**

Moving forward

As you interact with the ideas shared with you throughout this book, you will learn how to coach yourself to deal with changes that you want to make that you have identified by filling in the wheel of life and the pre-coaching questionnaire.

understanding
change

If you have now identified that you want to make a change, it is helpful to understand change in the first place. The main thing to remember is that you can only change yourself. If you want to see changes in your life that are dependent on other people making a change, or on some external factor changing, then you are liable to be disappointed. This happens when you say to yourself 'I will be happy if ...':

- I buy myself something (alias retail therapy)
- I change my hairstyle
- I change my wardrobe
- I change my body size
- I change my car
- I change my house
- I change my job
  - I change my partner
  - I change my teeth, nose, or other body parts
  - I change my kids (not possible, not in the rules!)

The further you progress down the list, the fact that happiness still eludes you could be because you are looking for external solutions to an internal issue.

Case study: **Rachel**

Rachel was not happy because her partner did not pay her enough attention. In the end she decided that their relationship was not working because he was obviously never going to change, and she ended it. Rachel is an attractive young woman and before long she was in another relationship. However, after only three months, she began to feel exactly the same as she had done in her previous relationship. Her boyfriend just did not pay her enough attention.

The questions that Rachel could benefit from asking herself are:

- **What kind of attention do I want?**

- **What conversation do I need to have with my boyfriend? After all, he does not actually know how I feel, as I have never told him.**

- **What can *I* do to encourage him to treat me differently?**

Notice that all of these questions are focused on what Rachel can do, not what her boyfriend needs to do. Rachel has given her boyfriend the power to achieve her goal, but he does not realize it because she hasn't told him. Telepathy is not as common as some people would like it to be.

To 'own' her goal and to bring it back within her control, Rachel needs to ask herself what she can start doing in order to help her partner to understand her dissatisfaction. By instigating a conversation and taking some action (learning to be more assertive, maybe) she can encourage him to behave differently towards her.

Repeating patterns

You may be able to identify a pattern that keeps repeating itself in your relationships. If so, here are some of the questions you might ask yourself:

- **Who am I being in this relationship?**
- **What am I doing/not doing in this relationship?**
- **What am I bringing to this relationship?**

- **What do I want from this relationship?**

- **How much am I able to be myself in a relationship?**

- **What does being myself really mean to me?**

- **Do I have any relationships that I have outgrown?**

- **What do I want to do about these relationships?**

These types of questions are designed to encourage you to really reflect and search within yourself to discover the answers. Take your time to listen to what comes into your mind. If you were being coached, then, with your permission, your coach would feed back what he or she hears to gain clarity and move forward with what you are saying. When you are coaching yourself, you might capture your thoughts in one of several different ways:

- **on paper, with a pen or pencil**

- **by mind-mapping with coloured pens**

- **in your journal or diary**

- **with a tape-recorder**

- **with a camcorder.**

There may be other ways, so choose the one that you are most comfortable with.

Communicating with your partner

Once you have clarified your own thoughts and feelings, the next step is to communicate your feelings to your partner. Invite them to share their thoughts and feelings about your relationship with you. When two people sit down and truly listen and respond to each other's needs within a relationship, they can deal with the challenges that they might face because they are prepared to face them together.

Truly listening helps you respond to one another's needs

Inner happiness

If you are looking to make a change in order to become happier in your life, consider first that the key to long-term happiness is to create happiness from within. Inner happiness, peace, contentment, sense of fulfilment – call it what you want – comes from understanding what really matters to you in life and choosing to live your life in a way that honours this. Seeking to be happier in your life by focusing purely on changing your external environment may be short-term solutions to issues that need some internal enquiry.

Enjoy making changes

What is it about making changes in your life that can seem so difficult? If it were just a case of making a decision to change, you would surely be living your ideal life already. If change were that simple, then you would be in your ideal job, and living in your ideal house with your ideal partner. You would be your ideal weight, have your ideal bank balance and go on your ideal holidays every year. What is holding you back?

Understanding change can be a great help here. Making small changes is achievable – going to bed half an hour earlier so that you are not so tired in the morning, drinking more water each day – but even these can be hard to sustain. When it comes to bigger, life-changing decisions, then, what is going to happen?

Making any change involves a degree of uncertainty. If you are not comfortable with uncertainty, then you may find making decisions to change anything unsettling – the bigger the change, the more unsettling it can be. It is a bit like the 'grass is greener' syndrome. Making a decision to change inevitably involves choosing one thing over another. The decision to lose weight can involve deciding to eat fruit rather than chocolate, or going for a walk after dinner rather than watching television. Whenever you choose one option, you are losing all the others at that moment. If you find this sense of loss hard, then change can be difficult, but not impossible.

Moving towards your goal

Choose the option that is going to help you move one step towards your goal, and move on. You cannot keep all your options open all the time, but you can make a different choice another time. As long as it does not take you too far off track, then exercise your power to make decisions and to make changes rather than ignoring the issue. Choosing to eat in a way that helps you manage your weight most of the time does not mean that you can never taste chocolate again.

When you begin to consider more life-changing decisions, adopting a coaching approach will take you through a series of steps that support you to have confidence in your ability to make the right decision for you at any one time, and to release your unlimited potential.

Your past is not your potential

Looking forward

You can only ever make a decision based on the information that you have available at the time. Life is easy in hindsight; living life without regret is the secret. Coaching deals with the present and what you want to create for yourself in the future. You can learn from experience, but the message from coaching is never let the past limit what you believe you can achieve in the future.

In the pre-coaching questionnaire (see page 61), what did you write down for the goals that you have achieved so far in your life? If you don't feel that you have achieved any goals, then it is important to remember that it is never too late to make changes and to start achieving. Making the decision to change an aspect of your life is not dependent on how old you are, where you come from or what experience you have. Making a change is all about having a genuine desire to be different, to do things differently or to have a different life.

Weighing up the pros and cons

We tend to succeed in making changes only if the benefits are likely to outweigh the costs. Think about a change that you are considering making:

- **What are the pros and cons of making this change?**

- **Where are you on the scale of wanting to see a change but also wanting things to stay the same?**

For example, Harry is now 30 and overweight. He has reached a stage in his life when he really wants to find a partner with whom to share his life. He sees the benefit of looking and feeling better as one way of attracting a woman into his life. He feels that losing weight will give him more confidence in himself generally. This is motivating him to make changes. How he chooses to make these changes will play a large part in how successful he will be in the long term.

Sustaining your progress

Have you ever started off convinced that you want to make a change, but then struggled to *sustain* your motivation? This may have been because you were adopting the 'all or nothing' approach. You may have set yourself huge goals that you expected to achieve all in one go, and when you found this hard to do you gave up, believing it to be impossible.

Understanding what it takes to make a successful change can alter all that. Your inner coach is on hand to help you to break down large goals into smaller, achievable steps that you can take one at a time. Monitoring your progress is important and acknowledging each small success is what can keep your focus and your motivation level high.

Remember that, if you are looking to change a habit or particular type of behaviour, then relapse is normal. Once you allow for the odd moments when you may return to a previous habit or type of behaviour, then, instead of giving up, thinking all is lost, you can choose to be gentle with yourself. Choose not to listen to your inner critic. Changing a habit can take time and requires patience, tolerance and understanding. This is where it can be really important to be your own best friend.

You are now strengthening the picture of what your ideal life looks like to you. You will be able to appreciate the importance of understanding change, and how this understanding can support you to make successful and sustainable changes.

Taking small steps helps you to reach your goals

focusing
on the positive

Another key aspect in the process of building your ideal life is *how* you work on achieving what you want to create. Revisit the creative visualization that you composed at the beginning of this book (see page 13). Check that it is as clear as it was when you first created it. Listen to what you hear yourself or others saying. If you filled in the section in the pre-coaching questionnaire (see page 61) about a personal trait or habit that you want to change, with anything that indicates that you have a negative way of looking at things, then this is important for you and needs addressing.

Make sure that you are focusing on what you *do* want rather than what you *don't* want. What is the difference? As you set out to work on creating a better life, if you focus on what you don't want then you can end up creating the opposite of what you really intended. For example, you may know someone who always believes that the worst is going to happen, and somehow they seem to have more than their fair share of problems to deal with. Whether it is because they are looking out for problems and therefore can always find them, or that they are just unlucky, depends on whether you believe that you have any power to create and control your own future.

I believe that creating the kind of life that you want has little to do with luck and a lot to do with belief, planning and being prepared to take action – being in the right place at the right time. However, that comes from a combination of knowing exactly what you want in life, trusting your intuition and taking action, believing that you can succeed. People who operate in this way in their lives believe in synchronicity, not coincidence.

You create your own luck

Negative thoughts

When you tune into your thoughts, how do you hear yourself talking about your future? Your thoughts might run along these lines:

- I don't want any more debt
- I don't want to lose my job
- I don't want to work until I am 65.

By focusing on the negatives here, it can be more difficult to achieve something positive. Even if you change 'I don't want' to 'I want', a negative slant still remains while you continue to use words such as 'lose' and 'stop'. These are called hidden negatives. The following statements are an example of this:

- I want to lose weight
- I want to stop smoking
- I want to get rid of my overdraft.

Positive thoughts

When you are looking to visualize your ideal life, it really is worth taking the time to check out how you are describing it to yourself. Positive thoughts and feelings translate into positive behaviour and actions. Here is how you can turn some of the examples above into positive statements:

- I don't want any more debt *becomes* I can manage money
- I want to stop smoking *becomes* I am a non-smoker.

There is no need to start making statements that you can't relate to, such as 'I am fantastic with money'. Too much too soon and you could end up reactivating your inner cynic. Take it one step at a time. You *can* end up being fantastic with money after years of being in debt.

playing
roles

Each relationship that you have with another human being involves a role that you play. As human beings, we have a natural instinct to want to belong. Hence we seek membership of certain groups – family, workplace, church and school are just a few. Each group has roles that have evolved for a variety of reasons, such as mutual support, passing on traditions, protection, and so on.

We acquire roles in a variety of ways. Some are unavoidable, such as son or daughter, or else we would not be here. Others come from choice, such as teacher, artist, manager, wife or husband. Some, although usually by choice, can even come by accident – parent.

Defining your roles can help you to become clear about:

- **all the roles that you play**

- **maintaining a balance**

- **whether you want to or need to play these roles**

- **role conflict**

- **how to deal with this conflict.**

Remind yourself of what you wrote down when completing the pre-coaching questionnaire (see page 61) about the aspects of your life that you enjoy most and those you enjoy least, before you work through the rest of this section.

Identifying your roles

How many roles do you play in your life? Take your time and write them all down. Here are just a few roles to stimulate ideas: son, daughter, wife, husband, partner, parent, grandparent, cousin, niece, nephew, aunt, uncle, godparent, guardian, foster parent, friend, companion, work colleague, musician, manager, employee, sister, brother, teacher, peacemaker, politician, gardener, volunteer, provider, knitter, cook.

Don't restrict yourself to what you consider may be your essential roles, but list *every* role that you play. You may find it helpful to refer back to the wheel of life exercise (see page 60) in order to group roles into certain areas of your life, so that you can get an overview. This will be useful when you start to look at creating a balance between your various roles, spotting areas of conflict and dealing with them.

Another way of looking at this is to consider that most roles have subsets. Take the role of parent, for example. This can break down into the following, to name just a few:

PARENT ROLE

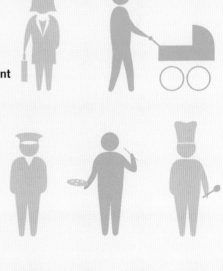

- manager
- peacemaker
- diplomat
- friend
- mentor
- homework consultant
- agony aunt/uncle
- chauffeur
- negotiator
- finance manager
- cook
- housekeeper
- referee
- nurse

Choosing your roles

Some roles are essential, others are optional, and some are predominantly someone else's expectation of you. Take a good look at your list. For each role that you play, describe in more detail who you are being within this role and what this role involves you doing. You may choose to be a work colleague and a friend with the same people. Consider who you are being and what you are doing that is the same and/or different when you are the friend rather than the work colleague.

Sometimes situations can dictate differences. You may not behave as a friend in exactly the same way with each of your friends, so what are the differences? Do you have different friends who appeal to different parts of your character? For example, there may be lively, chatty friends for when you feel outward-going, and a friend who prefers to have a quiet drink and a chat for when you are feeling more reflective. They may be one and the same, or they may not. What is important to recognize is whether or not you are behaving in a way that is being true to yourself in each of your roles.

- **Are you working in an environment that has a certain culture?**

- **Does this culture dictate how you have to be?**

- **Does this go against who you actually are so you have to behave in a way that is not really you?**

- **How stressful is this?**

How can you recognize if there is a conflict between who you are and a certain role that you play? Consider for a moment how you feel about some of your key roles and the relationships that exist within these roles.

- **How uplifted and fulfilled do you feel by this role?**

- **How drained do you feel by this role?**

- **Within each of your roles, which relationships drain you?**

- **Which relationships uplift you?**

- **In which relationships is there equal give and take?**

When you spend time in another person's company, all sorts of energy exchanges can take place. We talk about this in everyday terms when we say things such as 'I'm getting good/bad vibes (vibrations) from someone' or 'someone is/isn't on my wavelength'.

Crossed boundaries

Think of a relationship that is not successful for you. What part of the relationship does not work so well? How much energy do you put into it? How much energy do you receive in return? Here are a couple of situations that people have described to me.

Case study: **Peter and Chris**

When Peter received a phone call from his friend, it never lasted less than an hour and a half. Peter came off the phone feeling completely drained. It was almost as if his friend had plugged himself into a socket in Peter's ear and tapped into his energy. His friend went away feeling energized, but leaving Peter exhausted. Peter didn't know how to stop this happening.

Chris had a work colleague who used to come into her office 'just for a quick chat'. Half an hour later, he went back to his desk smiling, but Chris felt drained. She also knew that she would have to work late to catch up. She just didn't know how to stop this happening. Her colleague was always telling her what a good friend and a good listener she was. He never stopped to consider how she felt about his interruptions or the impact they had on her own time.

Can you relate to these situations? Is this a role you play for people? First, think about what boundaries are being crossed here and how it is serving you to play this role. If you are being drawn into playing a role that you would rather not play, the simple questions to ask yourself are:

- **What conversation needs to happen?**
- **With whom do I need to have this conversation?**

- **What am I going to say?**

- **When am I going to say it?**

You may feel, however, that you could never go through with the necessary conversation. If it were easy, then there would be no unsuccessful relationships and no crossed boundaries. So what holds you back from speaking your truth? What is important here is how you choose to have this conversation and who exactly you are choosing to be when you do.

Asserting yourself

Assertiveness is based on the belief that, whatever may have happened in the past that influenced your sense of self-worth, there comes a time when you can choose to believe that you are as important as any other person. The benefit of claiming your right to express your real feelings and opinions is that you live the life that you want to live, not the life that other people choose for you. The cost to you of denying yourself this right can be the release of a range of emotions from frustration or resentment to anger that can all generate negative stress. You still deal with situations, but from more extreme positions of either passivity or aggression, positions that are both actually manipulative.

You are just as important as anyone else

Passivity and aggression

The passive approach is self-effacing and apologetic: 'I'm hopeless at this – you can do it so much better'. This can be a learned helplessness. Cultural influence can still produce a social expectation that women are meek and self-effacing, while men must be commanding and decisive.

An aggressive approach might be: 'Like it or not, just do it'. In an office environment where those who 'make an impact' win promotion, a culture can develop where proving yourself right and others wrong is important. Making yourself look good at someone else's expense will score points. If you admire someone because they can dominate a meeting, while *you* find it difficult to put your viewpoint forward, you may both have more in common than you think – low self-esteem.

Choosing to be more assertive

Being more assertive isn't just about asserting your rights *all* the time. How can you use your sensitivity to look at a situation and invite yourself to respond appropriately? Take, for example, going to dinner with your partner's parents. You don't like them very much, but you choose to go with good grace. This is a sign of choosing to support your partner on such an occasion that comes from a strong relationship of give and take. You are not being a 'martyr'.

The tough question now is – how do you choose to behave? Being prepared to look at how you behave in certain situations and choosing to recognize your intentions creates a wonderful opportunity to strengthen your assertiveness. If you recognize that you are someone who needs to be liked by everyone, this can be counter-productive. This is rarely possible and can have a negative impact on your assertiveness. If, on the other hand, you have an approach that simply seeks to be fair, by using your negotiating skills on occasions, this can produce a positive outcome for everyone.

Using your voice, breathing and posture

Listen to your tone of voice. Is it balanced and even, cajoling or domineering? Do you feel calm, confident and open to the person that you are talking to? Another step towards becoming more assertive involves recognizing where tensions may lie in your body and how completely you use your breath when you are communicating. If you are not using your breath well, your voice can sound flat and unconvincing. This is not helpful when you want to communicate effectively with others. Your voice and your posture are powerful allies when you want to develop good rapport with people and command their respect in any situation. Stand in front of a mirror and observe yourself speaking.

- **What is your posture like?**
- **How 'centred' do you feel?**
- **How much do you use your mouth when speaking?**
- **How completely do you breathe in and exhale?**
- **What does your voice sound like?**

The Alexander Technique

Frederick Alexander developed an entire technique, now named after him, at the turn of the 20th-century. Alexander was an actor and public speaker. He lost his voice, and conventional medicine was unable to cure him. He decided to observe himself performing in front of a mirror. He soon noticed that he was not breathing properly and also realized that the strain of learning lines and performing was having an impact on his posture.

He was able to make the connection between the mind and body and in so doing adjusted his attitude and his posture, which helped him to regain his voice. He noticed other benefits such as increased confidence and presence when he spoke. He realized that the body is innately co-ordinated, but that we can develop unconscious habits that interfere with its natural functioning. Once we become aware of these, we can choose to correct them.

Changing your roles

Depending on how you choose to act in each of your roles, they can either be fulfilling or hindering to you in giving full expression to who you are. Personal effectiveness, happiness, self-esteem and a sense of fulfilment can all be influenced by how you relate to other people.

However, any changes that you decide to make can have a knock-on effect on those with whom you choose to live your life. Therefore exploring how this change might impact on others is important too, since it could be positive or negative depending on the change and how you choose to deal with it. What you are looking to create for *your* life can have some impact on the relationships that already exist. Ask yourself:

- **What change do I want to make?**
- **Who will it affect, and hence who needs to be involved in this change?**
- **How will it affect them?**
- **How will I honour and respect other people as I make this change?**
- **How do I plan to introduce the change that I want to make?**

NEW ROLE

Does your new role have a positive or negative impact on others?

Sorting out your roles

Take your time and enjoy exploring what being you really means to you. Think about how you could begin to sort out your roles to suit yourself better.

- **How do you change, if you change, with each role that you play?**
- **How much time do you get to yourself?**
- **How do you spend this time?**
- **How else would you like to spend this time?**
- **How comfortable are you with your own company?**
- **If you do not get any time to yourself, what needs to change to create this time?**
- **What conversation needs to happen?**
- **What outcome do you want?**
- **With whom do you need to have this conversation?**
- **What will you say?**
- **When will you say it?**
- **What is the next step?**

The next step

Coaching is all about taking small achievable steps.

- **Which roles do you choose to play and hence keep?**
- **Which roles do you choose to relinquish?**
- **Which roles do you want to modify to bring them into alignment with who you choose to be?**
- **Which relationships do you choose to keep?**
- **Which relationships do you choose to let go?**
- **Which relationships do you want to alter in order for you to be yourself?**

Case study: **Sarah**

Sarah had been married for 15 years. She had three wonderful children. Peter, her husband, was a good provider. They had got married straight after university. Looking back, Sarah knew that this had been a reaction to stepping out into the big wide world, and not wanting to be on her own. It was not that she was desperately unhappy, but she knew that she was not really happy either. They had had children in their mid-20s like all their friends and Sarah had poured her life into them ever since. As the years went on she could feel a growing sense of sadness that her relationship with Peter was empty. She had tried to explain to him that she longed for a hug or a cuddle occasionally, but Peter was not the 'romantic' type, as he put it, and often made fun of her about this. She had just accepted that fact and was getting on with it.

One day, however, it all just changed. Sarah knew that she could not continue to live her life as a mother, wife and daughter, but not as herself. She began to listen to herself and question what she wanted from life. She knew that she needed to make changes, changes that would affect a lot of people. However, by coaching herself through what mattered to her, what she believed about herself and her ability to make changes that respected those she loved, Sarah finally found the courage to discuss divorce with her husband. Although taken aback at first, Peter came to see that they were just going through the motions of a marriage and that they had both changed. Sarah and Peter divorced amicably and remained good friends and committed parents.

Five years later, their children are almost grown up and are happy, balanced young people. Peter is in a new relationship and Sarah married Jim last year. She feels completely herself and fulfilled.

changing your
relationships

If you have identified any roles and/or relationships that you would like to let go of or alter, your inner coach can be of use to you. It is probably fair to say that there are not many people who know exactly what is going on in your head. If the relationship you have within a role that you play is not as you want it to be, the challenge is to accept this fact and choose to do something about it.

Instigating a conversation with someone that is both respectful and honouring of them as a human being as well as you, in a calm and balanced way, can resolve many issues that generate stress in our lives. Taking positive action is far better than allowing situations to continue to annoy you. When one person finds the courage to tackle issues in this way, it is surprising how favourably even the most difficult of people can respond.

Case study: **Jenny**

Jenny, a single mother, has a 13-year-old son, Sam. In her words, Sam is 'getting in with the wrong crowd at school'. He has started smoking, and Jenny is worried that he could be drawn into taking drugs. Jenny has always had a good relationship with Sam, but over the last few months he has changed and no longer wants to talk with or listen to her. He spends his time at home in his room listening to loud music, does not do any homework and is positively sullen.

Jenny was doing her best to understand her son, but she was a *girl* when she was 13, and that was also in a different generation. No matter how hard she tried, it was impossible to really understand how Sam was feeling or what was going on for him.

Jenny decided to ask Sam how he wanted her to be with him as his mother now that he was 13. She also decided that, once she had asked the question, she would remain silent and concentrate on really listening to what Sam was saying. She had become aware in this process that she interrupted Sam quite regularly when they were talking. She waited until one day after school, when she sensed that Sam was in a happier mood, and they were alone together. She made a cup of tea and offered Sam one, which he accepted. She then started a conversation that went like this:

Jenny	**Sam**
Sam, do you mind if we have a chat just for a few minutes?	

Sam looked suspiciously at her, but eventually replied.

	What about?
How do you feel we get on these days?	
	OK, why?
I'd really like to know how you want me to be with you as your mum, now that you are 13.	

Sam looked at his mother for several seconds. Jenny remained open and silent.

	I'm not a kid any more and I don't want to be treated like a kid, which is what you're still doing.

Jenny resisted the urge to jump in and contradict what Sam had just said.

OK. I'll need your help to understand what that means to you. It's a long time since I was 13, and I was a girl as well.	

Sam laughed at this and Jenny sensed that he was starting to relax and engage with her in one of the most important conversations that she had ever had with him. An hour later, Sam gave Jenny a hug and thanked her for listening to him and clearly showing him that she wanted to understand how their relationship needed to evolve as he grew up. They agreed to do their best to talk over worries or concerns that either of them had, to negotiate and compromise when needed and above all to respect each other and to enjoy their relationship as mother and son.

Taking positive action is far better than allowing situations to annoy you

the importance
of TRUST

Where there is trust between people, there is tremendous strength. How does trust become established and sustained in any relationship? The word itself can be used as a helpful aide-memoire, standing for:

TRUTH

RESPECT

UNDERSTANDING

SPACE

TIME

Trust is a vital ingredient in the relationships that you choose to create with yourself. The impact of developing trust through truth, respect, understanding, space and time has far-reaching benefits, not only for you and all your relationships but also for society in general.

Truth

How difficult is it to tell the truth, either to yourself or to others? In recent years, phrases such as 'being economical with the truth' – meaning that you may not actually be lying, but are not telling the whole truth – have become part of our culture. How might such an attitude affect you in what you do or how you choose to interact in your relationships? Sometimes, it can be a case of not wishing to hurt someone's feelings, or thinking 'what they don't know won't hurt them'. Think, however, about a situation where you have promised to do something but you have over-committed yourself. This section will help you in making a decision to tell the truth properly, without feeling the need to excuse yourself.

Being 'true to yourself' can be defined as choosing to live your life with integrity. Think about what integrity means to you. This book is all about enjoying a good quality of life and choosing how you want to live *each* day. So, if you are stressed and exhausted, trying to fit in more than you can actually comfortably manage, what message are you giving yourself?

When I am working with a new client to plan what they want to achieve in their lives, the truth matters. Being truthful about the current reality in your life is vital if you want to move forward. If you get the feeling that you were not truthful with yourself when you were filling in the pre-coaching questionnaire (see page 61), then go back now and make any necessary changes. Being completely truthful with yourself about what you are doing or not doing is a great place to start if you want to change any aspect of your life. The questions to ask yourself are:

- **When my life is working, what is working about me?**

- **When my life is not working, what is not working about me?**

Without being judgemental, but simply by being truthful, you can take responsibility and choose to change. Being non-judgemental and unconditional is important when you are working with yourself, and equally when you are in a relationship that you want to improve, as this encourages others to speak their truth without fear of being thought less of.

Coaching works in the present, which eliminates the need for excuses. It involves thinking 'this is where I am right now – where do I want to go from here and how do I intend to get there?'. I believe that being truthful and positive builds respect for yourself as well as between you and other people.

Respect

When we look around us at what nature has created, we see amazing diversity. No two human beings look the same, unless they are identical twins. Even then, their personalities can be very different. Recognizing diversity first, and then respecting the differences that individuals possess, are important steps in building relationships. By respecting others, you will gain respect.

- **Choose a successful relationship and list the ways in which you show that person respect.**

- **Choose an unsuccessful relationship and list the ways that showing respect could improve that relationship.**

It is important not to treat people like children – deciding what is best for them, directing them, assuming you know better than they do. This can happen with the best of intentions. The underlying assumption is that a person cannot live their lives without you. If they did, where would that leave you?

Treating people like children is a type of behaviour that is difficult to interrupt, since it is done in the name of being supportive and 'on their side'. It is subtle and unconscious. 'I just want the best for you, that's all.' 'I just want you to succeed.' We can't do this to someone and give him or her profound levels of respectful attention at the same time. This is particularly important when dealing with young people.

Respect is enhanced with openness and honesty. Respecting other people's values and beliefs builds a strong relationship. Respecting yourself is about believing that you do know how you want to live your life and that you do not need to be told what to do. An age-old wisdom tells us to treat other people as we would wish to be treated ourselves. Those people who invest in this simple truth hold the key to wonderfully fulfilling relationships.

Empowering children

It takes a while before babies can do things for themselves, but then it is wonderful to watch their sense of achievement as they begin to master more and more of their world. On the other hand, they feel a sense of frustration if adults around them do not believe they are capable and keep insisting on doing things for them. When parents complain that their children refuse to do anything for themselves, they may be reaping the rewards of creating that dependency. When children are brought up to have responsibility for themselves, as soon as they are able, then they grow into balanced and confident young adults who understand the consequences of their actions as well as their rights. This is helping them to access authentic power, not 'pester power'.

It is never too late to make changes, though. If you have children who have become demanding and you feel that you are being expected to do more than is reasonable for them, they could benefit from being coached. Think about how you could implement the ideas in this book in your relationship with them. When young people feel truly listened to, with their views being consulted and respected, they can respond well to changes that need to be made for the good of the whole family.

Understanding

Coaching assists you to understand your values and beliefs. When you show understanding of the values and beliefs of other people, you can interact in a way that honours them. Showing yourself that you truly want to understand what matters to you enhances your self-esteem. Showing another that you genuinely want to understand what matters to them and how they feel develops a strong foundation on which to live life. In this sense, understanding is akin to empathy.

Notice the difference between understanding how another person might be feeling and believing that you know how they feel. It is not possible to know exactly how another person is feeling. Even if you have had a similar experience, such as going through a divorce or suffering a serious illness, each person's experience is unique to them.

Coaching supports an understanding of the various roles that you play and assists you to plan accordingly, so that you can enjoy all aspects of your life *and* achieve your goals. Understanding can therefore also involve honouring your need for space, as well as giving others space.

Space

Physical, mental and emotional space are all equally important in making a decision that could profoundly alter your life for the better. Giving yourself space goes a long way to reducing the risk of 'impulse buying' life. If you are looking to change your job, or if you have been made redundant, finding the space in your head to discover what matters to you is essential. Gathering all the information that you need to make a sound decision about your future is equally important despite the possible feelings of panic about the future that push you to 'firefight' the situation.

However, beware the inner characters, or even real people, who can invade this space, who are sometimes called 'dream stealers'. These are people who listen to your dreams only in order to try to take them away from you. I call this the 'trench mentality'. If we all sit in a trench together, it doesn't matter how cold, wet and miserable it might be, because at least it is the same for all of us. Yet, if one person has the courage to look over the side and see a better future out there, and goes for it, that puts pressure on the rest to do the same or risk feeling that they are missing out. These feelings can be very uncomfortable, so if they stop that person going anywhere they can avoid having to make the effort to change.

What choice do you have here? You can give in and fall back down into the trench, or you can coach yourself up and out. A coaching approach involves asking yourself what is best for you and supporting yourself in a thinking environment – one where you are doing the thinking. You create an energizing, special space where you can plan your future.

Find the space to discover what matters

Time

When you are planning what you are going to do, which tense do you use for the action words? If they are stated in the future tense, you need to appreciate that tomorrow never comes. All you have is now – the future does not exist. Consider making the decision to start a diet tomorrow. What's wrong with right now? If you have gone through the stage of contemplating a change, and you are committed to what you say you want to do, then there is no time like the present.

What is stopping you adopting a 'do it now' approach to life? Many people would answer this question by saying that they simply don't have enough time, and this is usually accepted as a fact. It is fair to say that, nowadays, people don't have to think about what they are doing, because they are too busy doing it. This can translate into the sense of urgency in life that is often deliberately created, as if it is a good motivator. If you do enough of something, then you are bound to succeed, because doing something is what produces results, isn't it? Not always.

If you actively listen to what this means to you, then you can work out how to address this challenge and do something about it. Coaching supports and encourages you to trust yourself that you *can* decide what to do about a situation, given enough time. Coaching creates an environment that supports you to think for yourself. In fact, urgency can prevent you from thinking clearly and working out for yourself how best to live your life. Reflective time allows your mind to explore endless ideas and creative thoughts.

Being true to your word, which is another aspect of living life with integrity, requires the determination to maintain a balance in life so that you do not end up over-committing yourself and then letting people down. If you say that you will do something by a certain time, and you plan your time so that you can achieve this, people will quickly grow to trust and respect you.

core
values

Truth, respect and understanding represent what we can call core values. Laying the foundations for your ideal life involves understanding what really matters to you. Take time now to explore this important area and refer back to your pre-coaching questionnaire (see page 61) as you work through this section.

Why is it so important to understand what your values are in life? I believe that our values make us who we are. What we value determines what life means to us and what actions we take. When we honour our values, on a regular and consistent basis, life is good and life is fulfilling.

Where values originate

Some values have been with us since our early childhood. We may have acquired them within our family, educational establishments, religion or peer groups. Often we are unaware that we have these particular values, because they come to our attention only when they are challenged in some way. An example of this could be that you are asked to do something and, at a conscious level, you agree and say yes, but when it comes to putting it into practice you feel uneasy about doing it.

Taking the time to understand what is important to you and to the people in your life enables strong and long-lasting relationships to build. When values and beliefs are known and honoured, setting goals becomes a natural process. When values, beliefs and goals are in alignment, this is an unstoppable combination, since values are 'primary motivators' (sources of true and lasting motivation).

On the other hand, when values are dishonoured, stress occurs. Identifying your values and beliefs helps you to remember that you are empowered and that there is no single, correct way to live life – there is only your way that works.

Becoming aware of your values and beliefs can also help you to understand what might be holding you back, enabling you to begin to choose how you want to behave in any situation. This will increase your confidence as well as the fun in your life.

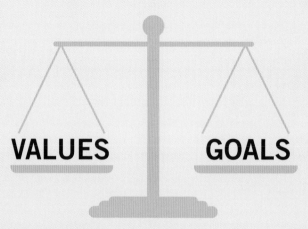

Identifying your core values

Discover some of *your* core values now by asking yourself what really matters to you in life. Recall a time when things were going well for you and then write down what comes to mind:

- **What were you doing?**
- **What feelings did you have that told you things were going well?**
- **What core values were being fulfilled here?**

Now recall a time when things were not going so well:

- **What was happening here that was different from the time above?**
- **Which core values were being dishonoured here?**

Here are some further questions to help you identify your core values:

- **When you are celebrating your 90th birthday, what do you want to celebrate about your life?**
- **What are you doing when you feel most content?**
- **What inspires you to take action?**

Clarifying your priorities

Take time to clarify what your values mean to you. For example, it may be your family that matters most to you. 'Family', however, is more of a 'chunk word' than a core value. A chunk word is a word that can hold different meanings for different people – such as 'work', 'hobbies', 'fun', 'family', 'partner', 'home'. Probing deeper with the question 'what does family represent to me?' can bring out different answers. One answer might be 'sharing or providing', whereas another might be 'spending more time together'.

Exercise:
Find your values cycle

Complete this cycle in the same way as you did the wheel of life (see page 60). Fill in each segment with one value that is important to you – for example, honesty. Then decide how much this value is being honoured in your daily life and shade in each section accordingly. If a scale helps, then the centre of the circle is 0 and represents 'hardly ever' and the outer edge is 10, representing 'all the time'. Now, in each segment, expand your thoughts by adding some notes about what this value means to you.

Here is an example:

In the first case, you might be looking to provide more for your family, so think about what you could do to earn more money. Doing a job that takes you away from your family, or spending more time working, to generate more income, is not stressful for you because you know that you are honouring your value of providing more for your family.

In the second case, if you are someone whose value is 'connectedness', meaning that you thrive on being with your family as much as possible, working means spending more time away from them, which may generate stress. You can coach yourself to think creatively as to how you can work more effectively, or even what job change you need to effect. To contain your working activities within an acceptable time scale and still leave enough time to spend with your loved ones is important to your well-being.

Coaching can help honour values, while creating a fun way of living a life that works for each individual since everyone is unique and special in their own way.

Case study: **Stephen**

Stephen completed the values cycle exercise and found that he valued his health above all else. What mattered to him was that he had a sense of well-being. When he stopped to work out exactly what that meant, he came up with the following statements:

- **I go to the gym three times a week.**

- **I drink two litres of water per day.**

- **I leave work on time every day.**

- **I spend one evening a week with friends, which is filled with laughter.**

- **I eat fresh food whenever I can.**

By working out what 'well-being' actually meant to him, Stephen ended up producing the above list of goals. In this way, identifying your values will give you a clear understanding of what goals to set that you really are motivated to keep.

Honouring your values

Once you have written down what each value actually means to you, then you can check what you are currently doing to honour each value by asking yourself the following questions:

- **How am I expressing my values in my life at the moment?**
- **Are any of my values being dishonoured?**
- **If so, what needs to happen to change this?**
- **How does my work honour or dishonour my values?**

Reflect for a moment on your current wheel of life (see page 60). How does the balance between your work/career area and all the other areas of your life look?

Your work–life balance

What motivates you to get up in the morning? Is it the knowledge that you have a fulfilling job and you also have something enjoyable to look forward to when work is finished? Or are you one of those people who has to drag themselves out of bed? How would you feel if, every day of your life, you looked forward to what that day had in store for you? If your work–life balance is not as you want it, think about what simple steps you could take to move towards better balance. Look at John's case study.

Case study: **John**

John was 40 and married with two small children. He was tired of the poor quality of life that he and his family endured. John's day was one long rush. He got up at 6am, struggled through the traffic and worked late most nights. John arrived home after the children had gone to bed. He sat in front of the television to eat a meal (often a takeaway since John's wife Judy also worked full time), before collapsing into bed, ready to do it all again the next day.

John could have had to do this for another 25 years or more (since his pension wasn't looking too healthy). In that time, he would probably have changed his job several times (owing to promotion, redundancy and so on); nevertheless, the underlying pattern was not going to change unless John decided to change it.

John's inner coach helped him to discover what really mattered to him in life. The first step was to identify his core values. One of John's first thoughts was his family. His inner coach probed deeper to help John understand what the word specifically meant to *him*. When John had to work late, he felt stressed because he valued the time he spent with his family and, increasingly, there was less of this.

Eventually, John had a list of eight values: fun, honesty, love, feeling connected, integrity, well-being, respect, creativity. John used the values cycle (see page 91) to help him get a picture of how much he was honouring his values in life. He realized that 'feeling connected' was very high on his list of values, but he was not expressing this in his daily life. He decided to address this problem.

John realized that he was also not expressing his creativity. He used to enjoy restoring antique furniture, something that he had not had the time or energy to do for several years. John and Judy sat down one evening to discuss their options for bringing a better quality of life to the entire family. They came up with all sorts of ideas. Then John realized that what he really wanted to do was to have a go at establishing a business restoring antique furniture. Judy listened, without interrupting him, while he explained what that would mean to him. She could sense his enthusiasm.

They began to explore how they could make his dream a reality, and what impact it would have on the rest of the family. John had been successful in his career so far, but now the price they were all having to pay was too great. Judy had gone back to work once the children started school because she loved teaching, but that was also now demanding too much time and energy. As a result of their efforts, they lived in a very large, attractive house. After many discussions, and a visit to a small-business advisor, John handed in his notice at work, and they sold their house and bought a property with an outbuilding that would make an ideal workshop. They had a lump sum left over, which they invested in a pension fund.

John still works hard, but he is enjoying every minute because he is working from home and seeing much more of his family. Judy is benefiting because John is happy to take over more of the management of the house. He has discovered how much he enjoys cooking, another outlet for his creativity. Two years on, John has a solid business and a fantastic quality of life.

raising your
self-esteem

Self-esteem, the value we place on ourselves, can affect our ability to make changes. Though most people can cope with factors such as loss of job, bereavement, retirement, poor health or stress which affect self-esteem, these can throw others into emotional confusion. William Stewart concluded, in his book *Building Self Esteem*, that there are three categories of people with self-esteem issues:

1	People who are usually confident and self-assertive but whose self-esteem has taken a knock	Unexpected events such as job loss can come along and attack even the most confident person and lower their self-esteem.
2	People who have a consistently low self-esteem	These people never think of themselves as having any worth. This may result from them having had more negative than positive inputs from almost the moment they were born. Finding any pleasure in life can often prove very challenging for them.
3	People who find refuge in their role at work	We all know people who need to be needed. They are respected for their contribution to society, and this is how they feel they are worth something. The moment they leave work, however, a sense of worthlessness can arise. Without work, they almost cease to exist. People with work-related self-esteem are particularly vulnerable, especially nowadays when there is no job security. When the job goes, their self-esteem goes with it.

Exercise: **Measuring your self-esteem**

In the pre-coaching questionnaire (see page 61), how easy did you find it to answer the question 'What are your natural gifts/abilities?'? If your answer is 'not very', then this exercise is for you. When you are being coached or coaching yourself, it is very important to understand where you are on the self-esteem spectrum. This can contribute enormously to how well you set about taking action to achieve your goals. So, if you want to find out more about your own self-esteem, then take a few minutes to respond to the following statements by putting a tick in the most appropriate column on the right.

	OFTEN	SOMETIMES	SELDOM
I have positive expectations of my efforts			
I can accept responsibility when things do not work out			
I can acknowledge myself for my part when things do work out			
I am happy with my life			
I am anxious about my life			
I am prepared to take risks			
I experience positive emotions			
I feel equal to other people			
I engage in self-development activities			
I appreciate and show gratitude for the good things in my life			

If your ticks are predominantly in the 'often' column, then you have high self-esteem. On the other hand, if they are predominantly in the 'seldom' column, this indicates that coaching could be very helpful in assisting you to build your self-esteem.

Coaching yourself to raise your self-esteem

As we have seen, coaching does not deal with the past. So, if you have recognized, or established, that you have a lower self-esteem than you would like, looking back to where this may have come from – childhood, peer group, experiences at school – is not what coaching is about. Coaching deals with the now and the way that you choose to be in the future.

High self-esteem is about putting a positive value on yourself. *Low self-esteem* results from attaching negative values to yourself, or part of yourself. If your self-esteem is low, then the question is 'what are you choosing to do now?'. Starting to build a stronger self-esteem comes from raising your awareness, understanding yourself better and deciding who it is that you want to be in your life. If some of your initial ideas about your sense of self-worth were influenced by an education system that recorded ability predominantly through literacy and numeracy, then consider how you feel about your other kinds of intelligence (see the box on Multiple intelligences, page 98).

What you believe about yourself from what others have told you may bear no relation to your true ability. Have a go at answering the following questions:

- **Which 10 things make you special?**

- **Which 10 things do you do well? (Even if it is 'I clean my teeth well', you can always find something!)**

- **What makes you unique?**

- **Which 10 things are you grateful for?**

If you end each day with a list of things that you are grateful for, this is a positive way to maintain a healthy self-esteem.

Multiple intelligences

Multiple intelligences have been recognized by many people working in the area of learning and personal development. Notable among them are Howard Gardner, Daniel Goleman (author of the book *Emotional Intelligence*) and Danah Zohar (co-author of the book *Spiritual Intelligence*). The exact number of different intelligences and their labels varies depending on whose work you read, but here is a summary.

- **Literacy** – how comfortable are you with words, reading and writing?

- **Numeracy** – do you enjoy numbers, logical, systematic thinking?

- **Spatial intelligence** – can you see the whole picture, visualize an outcome?

- **Physical intelligence** – are you well co-ordinated, naturally good at physical activities?

- **Musical intelligence** – do you have an appreciation of sound and the effect it has on human emotion?

- **Natural intelligence** – do you possess an awareness of the inter-connectedness of humans and their environment?

- **Interpersonal intelligence** – do you get on well with others, display natural empathy?

- **Intrapersonal intelligence** – how well do you know yourself, understand yourself?

- **Spiritual intelligence** – do you sense that the physical world is not all that there is?

using the
SMART model

As you learn to activate your inner coach, use a simple process to structure your thoughts. It is really important to be clear about your goals and using the SMART model can support you to do this:

SPECIFIC	What do you really want to achieve?
MEASURABLE	How will you measure your progress?
APPEALING	How inspiring to you is this goal?
REALISTIC	How realistic is this goal? This is a reality check that does not limit achievement.
TIMED	By when do you want to have achieved this goal?

Case study: **Rebecca**

Rebecca desperately wanted to lose weight. Every time she started on a diet, however, it lasted about three days before her willpower caved in and she was back to her old eating habits. Rebecca then felt despondent, and so ate even more than she usually did, with disastrous results – she put on even more weight. Rebecca was listening only to her inner critic. What she heard was: 'You are weak-willed and pathetic – if celebrities can achieve fabulous figures even straight after having babies, why can't you?' Rebecca's self-esteem was pretty low.

Rebecca's inner coach, however, believed totally in her ability to achieve anything that she really wanted for her life, and was there to encourage and support her to break down her goals into manageable steps and to take them one at a time. In this situation, her inner coach helped by using the SMART model to help Rebecca work out what she wanted:

SPECIFIC	To be able to fit into her smaller-sized clothes again.
MEASURABLE	To let her clothes tell her how she was progressing. She decided not to weigh herself every day as a measure, as small fluctuations upwards upset her and had triggered her into giving up in the past.
APPEALING	To look and feel really great in a bikini on her summer holiday.
REALISTIC	To start immediately, since that would give her six months to adjust her weight down by the required amount.
TIMED	To be her desired size by 30 June so that she could enjoy choosing a new bikini before her holiday which was to start on 12 July.

Rebecca really wanted to stay focused on her goal. She decided to pin on her kitchen wall a picture of herself when she was slimmer as a positive reminder and motivator that she could look like that again – a good boost for her self-esteem. If the going got tough, she knew that the answer was to call upon her inner coach, who would continue to encourage and support her.

Rebecca's inner coach listened only to what *was* working, not to what wasn't working, and encouraged Rebecca to focus on looking for the positive evidence that she could succeed and not the negative evidence that she might have looked for in the past. If Rebecca had the odd relapse, her inner coach reminded her not to judge herself and that, when looking to make changes, relapse is normal. If she allowed for that and kept going, then she would achieve her goal.

What needs to happen for you to expect success?

Consider the following questions:

- **What activities can you plan each week that you will look forward to?**
- **What needs to happen for you to allocate your time each week to avoid tensions and stress?**
- **What do you want to read or listen to each week to encourage positive thoughts?**
- **How independent are you in your thinking and your decision-making?**
- **If your answer is not very, what needs to happen to increase your independence?**

Notice how the listening and questioning skills covered in the first part of this book are now coming together with a positive purpose.

the 'house of change'

Here we are going to look in more depth at the relationship between change, thoughts, feelings and behaviour. The situation in which a change is planned can prove to be an extra challenge, particularly if you have no support.

The 'house of change' diagram shows the relationship between the different components involved in change. You can see that the work that you have already done on clearing the ground has identified your beliefs. Understanding your values supports you to build your life on strong foundations.

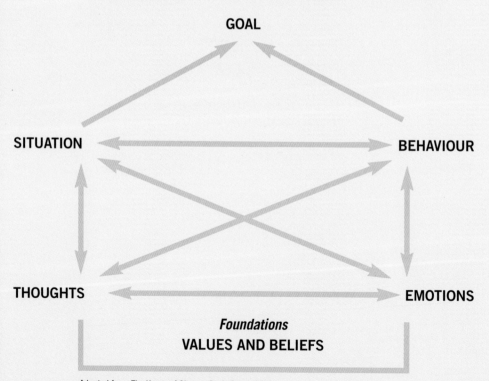

Adapted from *The House of Change*, Dr. A. Grant, 2002

If you are looking to make real and lasting changes in your life, you need to address all the four corners of your 'house'. Changing just one area may not give you the results that you seek in the long term. If you change your behaviour but you continue to listen to a negative inner character, you will ultimately find it difficult to keep going and you then risk giving up. For example, say you decide to go jogging after work three times a week in order to get fitter. If you keep listening to an inner voice that says 'you'll never keep this up', it will probably last only a week before you do give up.

Coaching can help you become a master builder

On the other hand, if you change only your thoughts and feelings, but your behaviour remains the same, then no real change will result. For example, in winter you might decide that you will start putting some money aside for your summer holiday so that you will have enough spending money to really enjoy yourself for a change. Unfortunately, you never actually do anything about it, so, when summer comes and you are on your way to your destination, you know that you will have to be careful and watch what you spend, as usual.

'Rome was not built in a day', so when you are looking to make changes remember to give yourself the space and time to do it. When you set out to build a house, each stage is crucial for the success of the overall project. If you skimp on the foundations, your house could subside. If you do not check the alignment of the four walls, the roof won't fit. 'Cowboy' building can result in your house collapsing.

Building your ideal life

Now you are ready to take the picture of your ideal life and construct each aspect of it every day. After initially describing a useful coaching model for you to follow, this section is designed to show you how you can coach yourself to make significant and sustainable changes in eight key areas of your life, which equate to the headings in your wheel of life (see page 60):

- *physical environment*
- *personal growth*
- *money*
- *family*
- *relationships*
- *fun and leisure*
- *work and career*
- *health and fitness*

If, in the wheel of life exercise, you chose different headings from the ones used here, refer back to them when reading through the relevant section. Even if you are completely happy with a certain area, consider reading about it anyway, as this may prompt you to take a fresh look. It can certainly help you to maintain a balance as you make adjustments to other areas.

As you work through the different sections of your wheel of life, you will begin to see how one section does not stand in isolation from any other. If you want to make a change in your work life, it may involve an aspect of self-management and/or personal growth. Choosing to change simultaneously where you work and live could have a positive impact on your financial position and leisure time too. Each section of the wheel of life represents the building blocks to constructing your ideal life.

Finding abundance

Before you start, it may be helpful to give some thought to the concept of *abundance* and what this means to you. Abundance is not just about money – it is about unlimited potential and possibilities in every aspect of life. In the 21st century, some people are changing their lives to reflect that money is not what makes them happy. A quality of life with less pressure to earn big salaries is sought by more and more people. What you earn, or your job title, does not define you or bring you guaranteed happiness. You define yourself through your values, what you stand for and whom you choose to be in your life. True happiness comes when you are living your life in alignment with your values.

What evidence of abundance do you have in your life already? Looking for the positive evidence that you have abundance is a good place to start. If at first you feel that you cannot find any evidence, then consider where you are looking. Remember that what you focus on is what you are indicating to yourself you want more of. If you have a challenge accepting that you deserve abundance in your life or you focus on your lack of abundance or scarcity, then you are not likely to suddenly start achieving abundance. Notice what abundance you have in a loving family or friends, books to read, music to listen to, food, clothes, flowers in a garden – the list can be endless.

We live in a world of abundance and yet some people have more than others, and in some cases vastly more. What will you do when you have more than enough? In order to be able to share out abundance, you need to be able to draw it in first. By looking after your own well-being financially as well as physically, mentally, emotionally and spiritually first, you are enabling yourself to look after others if you choose. You have the power to help redistribute abundance. As you begin now to focus on coaching yourself, you may discover that there is a wider contribution that *you* eventually want to make.

Happiness comes from within

the TGROW
model

Before you start on changing specific aspects of your life, here is a useful coaching model that you can employ with any goal. The model, that your inner coach can help you work through any time you want, was first promoted by Sir John Whitmore in the late 1980s. It has stood the test of time as a very effective tool to unleash potential, keep focus and gain commitment to achieving goals. TGROW stands for:

TOPIC GOAL REALITY OPTIONS WAY FORWARD

Work through the model below to see how easy it is to use to help you structure your thoughts on any topic.

TOPIC
Which area of your life would you like to work on right now? You may find it helpful to look back at your wheel of life in order to select an area of your life that you feel needs a change or can be improved.

GOAL

Establishing a clear goal is essential in any coaching conversation. Remember, a coaching conversation is not just a chat that gives you a nice, warm feeling. It is a dynamic, focused conversation designed specifically to produce an action with a positive outcome. Visualizing your goal (see page 13) may be a method that works for you. Running your goal through the SMART process (see page 99) is also a good way to check that this goal is important enough to you to motivate you to take action.

Remember, too, that you can set goals only for yourself. It is no good setting a goal such as 'I want my children to do their homework without me having to nag them'. You could look instead at coaching them to achieve this. What is the specific goal that you really want to achieve? Can you state your goal in one short, positive sentence?

REALITY

Now that you have a clear idea of your goal, establish the current reality. What is the current situation in more detail? Remember, your mind has the capacity to handle many things but it cannot do that if you present it with non-reality and untruths. Once you have a clear idea of where you are starting from, you can explore options to move yourself forward.

Notice that you have decided on your goal before exploring reality, just as in this book you created the picture of your ideal life before starting to examine your current reality. This is done for a very good reason. Choosing a goal first is free from any constraints that you might put on yourself from what is going on in your life right now. You can explore your unlimited potential.

If you find that conversation with your inner coach is being interrupted by the obstructive travelling companions that you identified earlier, remind yourself of the tactics you looked at to silence them and keep practising them.

When describing your current situation in more detail, remember to be completely honest.

- **What have you done so far?**
- **What has been the effect of your actions?**
- **What has held you back before?**
- **How will you deal with this differently now?**
- **Who can support you?**
- **What does it take for you to remain non-judgemental, encouraging and supportive of yourself as you answer these questions?**
- **If you have done nothing so far, what positive information does that give you?**
- **How can this help you to check that you are working on the right goal?**

OPTIONS

This is the place to be very creative and have a lot of fun. Do not dismiss any idea that comes to you at this stage. An idea that may sound foolish at first can trigger your mind to produce another more viable option. You won't know if something is possible, ultimately, until you have a go.

- **What ideas do you have to achieve your goal?**
- **If money were no object, what do you see yourself doing?**
- **What could you do to move yourself one step towards your goal?**

Notice the term *one step*. Some people expect to achieve their goal in one giant leap and, if they cannot, they give up. Coaching shows you how to break goals down into small, achievable steps.

- If you knew you could do anything, what would you do?
- What else can you think of? Keep asking yourself this question until you really have exhausted all your ideas.
- Which idea excites you most?
- Who can support you?
- What do you want them to do or say?
- What conversation needs to happen?
- When will you have this conversation?
- What obstacle might get in the way?
- How will you overcome this?

Every journey starts with the first step

WAY FORWARD

Now you are ready to plan exactly what you are going to do. What are you actually committing to doing? When are you going to start? It is crucial to get a clear answer to this question. Have you ever dreamt of doing something but without setting an actual start date? The result is that no action actually takes place.

If appropriate, ask yourself more questions that start with what, where and how. Keep going until you are completely clear in your mind what needs to happen for you to achieve your first goal.

Check out how excited you are about this goal. Is it a case of 'I can't wait to get going'? You could use SMART again (see page 99). If this goal is not appealing to you and you are not that excited, then, instead of setting yourself up to fail, simply rerun the process until you find a goal that does inspire you enough.

TGROW as a cycle

In his book *Effective Coaching*, Myles Downey shows TGROW as a cycle rather than a linear model:

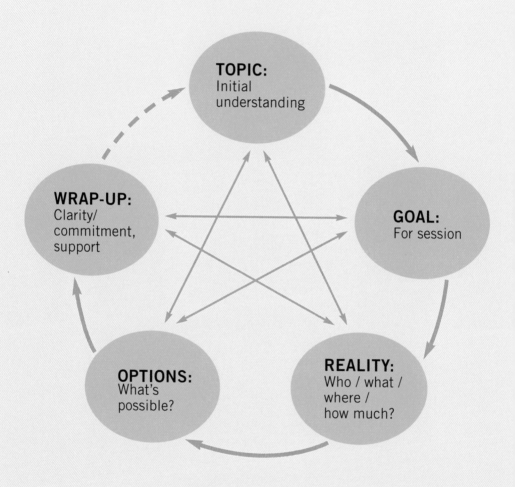

The only difference in his version from that described is that he refers to the final section as 'wrap-up'. You can see how easy it is to move between the stages until you arrive at *exactly* what you want to do.

Rewarding yourself

When you succeed, how do you plan to celebrate? Acknowledging yourself every step of the way is a powerful way to move towards living your ideal life. Here again, it is fun to be creative. Rewards do not have to cost money. For some people, giving themselves time to do something that they enjoy is the best reward – having a long, relaxing bath with candles and your favourite music, or watching sport in the middle of the afternoon while enjoying an ice-cold beer and *not* feeling guilty.

For people who work from home, planning a picnic lunch in the park or a trip to the countryside as a break can be a wonderful reward. This also reinforces your power to choose a quality of life for yourself. What will you do or give yourself as a reward for your efforts?

Using the TGROW model

In each of the eight topics that follow, there is a section entitled 'Using TGROW'. These sections are designed to work mainly by providing you with a list of the most relevant questions to be asking yourself at each stage of the process. The rest is up to you and your inner coach.

Acknowledge yourself every step of the way

physical
environment

When you set out to build the life of your dreams, having enough physical and emotional energy to enjoy the process is important. The place that you call home and where you choose to retreat from the outside world for certain periods can tell you a great deal about what is going on in your life at any one time. Your external physical environment can be a fairly accurate outward representation of your inner self – the best mirror that you can buy. However, it is a two-way mirror, since your home environment also has an effect on you.

If you *have* to maintain a pristine home, could it be your way of feeling in control externally when your inner self feels quite the opposite? If you were brought up by overly demanding parents, do you *not* bother about your home because it is a form of rebellion representing an area over which you have control now? On the other hand, you could be living very happily in *organized chaos* because you are content with your inner self and who you are.

This section gives you the chance to look at how you are living and, if it is not as you want to live, decide to make changes. How did you feel about your physical environment when you filled in your wheel of life (see page 60)? What part did your physical environment play in the picture of your ideal life? There are lots of television programmes, magazines and books on how to create your ideal home environment. What needs to happen for you to implement what you watch or read? If you are going to spend your time in a place, why shouldn't it be uplifting, fun, peaceful – whatever you want it to be?

Now is the time to bring your dreams into reality. Here are some questions to start you off within the TGROW model (see pages 106–109) that can help to structure your thoughts. However, always go with your own intuition as to what is best for you if other thoughts and questions come up.

USING **TGROW**

TOPIC   – Your physical environment.

GOAL   – What kind of environment do you want to live in? Use the techniques that suited you to get a clear picture. Take your time to reflect on each room in your house or flat. Imagine each room exactly as the special space that you want it to be. Depending on the range of rooms that you have in your home – what do you want each room to represent to you? Work through the following list:

- **Bedroom**
- **Bathroom**
- **Kitchen**
- **Living room**
- **Dining room**
- **Children's room**
- **Office/study**
- **Utility room**
- **Other rooms**
- **Garage**

Coaching helps you to break down goals into bite-sized chunks, so visit one specific room to start with, say the bedroom. Use **SMART** (see page 99) to help you to clarify what you want this room to look and feel like. With the help of the questions below, coach yourself through any changes that you want to make to achieve your ideal for this room. If you have another room that you want to work on, just apply the same types of question and any others that you think of.

REALITY   – How would you describe your bedroom? Where are you at the moment? If you are at home, take a look around your bedroom. What do you see? If you are not at home, then imagine what you would see if you went into your bedroom as if you were visiting for the first time. Take a fresh look. We can become oblivious to things that can have a draining effect on us the longer we live with them and put up with them. Raising your awareness here gives you the choice to make changes if you want to.

- What do you value about your bedroom?
- How does this room help to honour your values?
- If you value peace and harmony, does this room offer you these when you spend time there?
- If a value, such as security, is dishonoured (you may have been burgled), what needs to happen to bring a renewed sense of security to your home and this room in particular?

When you are setting goals for yourself, always keep what matters to you most, namely your core values, in mind – they are powerful motivators. Ask yourself:

- How much time do I spend in this room?
- What can I see?
- What colours are in the room?
- What type of furniture is in the room?
- What sort of flooring do I have?
- What can I hear and smell?
- How much light is in the room?
- What else do I want in the room to make it a place in which I can enjoy spending my time?
- How much noise can I hear from outside?
- How do I feel when I walk into this room?
- How do I feel when I wake up in the morning?
- Have I slept well in a room that refreshes me?
- If this room is my retreat, what else do I want to create in this environment that supports me to reenergize myself each day?

OPTIONS
- Become as imaginative as you can and list all the ideas that you come up with to create your ideal for each room. Use questions such as 'if money was no object, what would I do or have?' or 'if I knew that I could do anything, how would I imagine this room?'. The possibilities are endless, so do not let your inner cynic, sceptic or critic join you for this exercise.

- What ideas do I have to create my ideal bedroom?
- If I want more space, what needs to happen to create this space?
- If I want more order in my bedroom, what can I do to achieve this?

- If I could create my ideal bedroom, what would I see myself doing?
- Who can support me to make the changes that I decide to make?
- What has stopped me making changes to this room in the past?
- What unhelpful inner character do I need to silence?
- What do I already have that I want more of?
- What do I have that I want less of?

WAY FORWARD
- Which option appeals to me most?
- What am I actually going to do?
- When am I going to do it?
- Who else needs to be involved in this change?
- When will I talk to them?
- What will I say?
- What obstacles could get in the way?
- How will I overcome them?
- What resources do I want to access to achieve my goal?

For all the rooms, consider the following questions:

- Who am I in relation to my clutter?
- How does it feel when I have had a good clear-out of clutter?
- If I could keep this room just as I want it, what do I see myself doing?

Decide how you will reward yourself when you have achieved your goal.

Clearing out clutter

Sometimes it is not a matter of making changes to a room but of choosing to *keep* the room how you want. Clutter can represent a range of feelings such as 'I can't cope', 'I am overwhelmed' or 'I give up'. Clutter can also symbolize:

- **unfinished business**

- **clinging to the past**

- **stagnant energy**

- **an unwillingness to change**

- **a belief in scarcity.**

Hanging on to clutter can deplete your energy and keep you stuck in life. Clearing out clutter means that you are telling yourself 'I can cope', 'I am in control'. By creating space, you are indicating that you trust that you will always have what you need when you need it.

Case study: **Craig**

Craig never put anything away. When he lived at home, his mother had always done it for him. Now he was in a flat of his own, it was disastrous. He spent so much of his time just trying to find things, he was now frustrating himself to the point where he knew that he had to take action. Instead of going out to the pub with his mates, he sat down one Friday night and thought about how he really wanted to live. Once he had this clear in his mind, he took an honest look at how he was actually living at the moment and decided to change.

He went out and bought a few storage boxes and spent the weekend sorting out his flat. Many bags of rubbish later, he was delighted with the transformation. The knock-on effect is that Craig has done the same at work. Now he spends less time trying to find papers that he has left lying in piles and more time hitting his deadlines. He doesn't have to work late nearly as often and he is finding time to go to the gym twice a week. So he is feeling really good in all sorts of ways he could not have foreseen, just because he made the decision to sort out his physical environment at home.

Your working environment

More and more people are either choosing to work from home or are being employed as home workers. This trend is likely to increase in the future. A major work–life balance opportunity exists for people who look to work from home. If this is an attractive option to you, what room or area in your home would enable you to create this reality for yourself? If you are self-employed and can relate to the case study about Helen below, then think about what needs to happen in your home for you to really enjoy working from home. It could be as simple as making sure your 'work' and 'living' spaces remain separate.

If you work outside your own home, however, take a look at your working environment. You can use exactly the same process to ensure that where you choose to spend a considerable amount of your time is as conducive to your physical and emotional well-being as possible.

Case study: **Helen**

Helen was self-employed and worked from home. There came a time when she felt low and de-motivated. Her business was not growing and she was finding it hard to achieve a good work–life balance. She decided to use coaching.

First, Helen decided what she wanted for her life – a thriving business and a work–life balance that would give her the energy and time to continue to build her business and enjoy life. She realized that her business did not have a separate place in her home, and hence almost every room had become her office. There was no place where she could switch off from her business. She answered the phone at all times of the day and night, not knowing whether it was a business or social call until she picked up the receiver. She never shut her business down in order to enjoy an evening off with her husband. No wonder she was feeling low.

What Helen felt inspired to do was to make structural alterations that would enable her to create a specific office area. She would have easy access to this area, but she could also contain all her business activities there and close it down at the end of a normal working day. She also decided to get a separate business telephone line with an answerphone, so that she could regulate her phone calls. These changes enabled Helen to claim back her home.

personal
growth

When we are born, each of us has a sophisticated 'computer' sitting in our head – the brain – but, unfortunately, there is no accompanying manual to tell us how to use it. Consequently, we all have a need to explore inside ourselves. This exploration is lifelong, because learning and understanding more about ourselves continue with each new phase of life that we enter.

We engage in this exploration out of a sense of intense curiosity about our unlimited potential rather than out of the belief that we are not good enough or not whole at the outset. The term 'personal growth' can be used to mean exploring and fulfilling your unlimited potential. What does 'personal growth' therefore mean to you, and how are you living your life in relation to this?

Life crises

A few years ago, there was much talk about the **mid-life crisis**. If you had not reached the top of your profession or achieved a senior position in your company by a certain age, then you felt that you had no future. This was capable of plunging hard-working, capable individuals into a depression or crisis. However, with very little job security these days, the mid-life crisis seems to have been largely forgotten.

The focus is turning more to the **pension crisis** – how will I manage financially when I want to stop work? Continuing to explore our unlimited potential may become overshadowed in later life by a return to meeting our basic needs such as food, housing and health care. Since we all have the potential to live longer, we will require increased funds to supply these needs in a period when a conventional income may have ceased and a pension may be linked to the vagaries of the global stock market. If you are in this phase of your life or contemplating this phase, then this section on personal growth may be helpful to explore your income-generating potential in a new way. The message here is that it is never too late. Mary Wesley published her *first* novel when she was 70.

More recently, a new term has emerged – the **quarter-life crisis**. If you are in your 20s, the challenge can be to discover what you really want to do to earn money while honouring your core values. Many young people are being encouraged to continue their education into their early 20s. So a degree of independence is achieved by leaving home, along with a sufficient structure to feel secure. Most young people know that their aim is to come out of university with a degree. However, if the nature of their degree is not vocational, such as training to be a doctor, then on leaving the safety of this institution many young people are still challenged with what it is they really want to do.

Maintaining independence can be a very real challenge when there may be student loans to pay off while affording rent or a mortgage. A lot of young people take on a job in order to start the journey of paying off debt rather than discovering what they really want to do. Once accustomed to money and a certain lifestyle, it is hard to be true to yourself when you ultimately discover what you believe your life purpose to be, if it is different from what you are actually doing. On the other hand, up to 25 per cent of young people in their mid-20s are either back living at home or receiving a financial contribution from their parents towards accommodation costs, and, ultimately, this has a negative impact on their self-esteem.

Changing work patterns

Another major impact on self-esteem for today's working generation is the loss of the permanent job contract. More and more people are forced to take on temporary contracts that can involve a resting period in between. Others find themselves working as full-time freelancers with no guarantees of long-term work. A range of feelings and emotions can emerge:

- **confidence takes a knock**

- **doubt sets in about the ability to do the job anyway**

- **self-esteem takes a dive**

- **depression can set in because there is little money with which to enjoy life**

- **life is on hold again.**

Consequently, more young people are delaying settling down as they seek to make sense of the world of work, to gain some financial stability before taking on the responsibilities of children, and to live a little. Focusing on personal growth can make a powerful contribution to building your ideal life despite changing work patterns. We have unlimited potential, and any limits that we believe exist are those that we place upon ourselves.

Reassessing your goals

Revisit your pre-coaching questionnaire (see page 61) and look at your original answer to the question 'what goals have you set aside as unachievable?'. No matter what your age, are you in the process of setting aside a goal at the moment? If so, now is the time to revisit your decision to check that it is the right one. For some people, a goal that is set aside as unachievable could be:

- **finding the right partner**
- **finding a more rewarding job**
- **starting up your own business**
- **moving abroad**
- **taking a holiday of a lifetime**
- **learning to swim**
- **learning a foreign language**
- **playing an instrument**
- **training to do a completely different job.**

Use some of the following questions to stimulate your thinking:

- **What did you want to be when you were growing up?**
- **What were you good at that you no longer have the time or the energy to do?**
- **What did you enjoy doing as a child?**
- **What do you want to accomplish in your life?**

Life can sometimes sweep us up like a fast-flowing river, and dreams can become left behind and forgotten. Living life without regret is the key to living your ideal life.

Coach yourself to achieve what you want for your own personal growth using the TGROW model. Answer the questions below, and listen for any other questions that your inner coach is coming up with.

TOPIC — Personal growth, whatever that specifically means to you.

GOAL — What is it that I want to do that I have not found the time to do yet, or I have ended up believing I could not achieve?
— If I knew that I could succeed, what would I see myself doing?
— What would I really like to see happen in my life?
— How is my self-management supporting me to achieve what I want?
— How do I want to utilize my natural gifts and talents more?
— What do I want my legacy to be?

REALITY — What has held me back from taking action on this goal?
— What stops me doing something now?
— What am I putting up with about myself, about others?
— What impact does my self-management have on what I can achieve?
— What roles do I want to play?
— What role do I want to relinquish?
— Who else needs to know about what I want to do?

OPTIONS — In what ways can I achieve what I want for my own personal growth?
— What do I see myself doing?
— In what ways can I improve my self-management?
— If I knew that I could do anything, what would I be doing?
— What other ideas do I have?
— What support do I want?
— What do I need to do to gain this support?
— How will I overcome any obstacles?

WAY FORWARD — What am I actually committing to do for myself?
— When am I going to start?
— How can I measure my progress?
— What resources do I need?
— How will I celebrate my achievements?

Acknowledging that you are gay

If you know that you are gay, but in order to achieve personal growth you want to find a way to tell those you love about it, you can coach yourself through what needs to happen for you to live your life in a way that honours and respects who you are. Ultimately, it comes down to deciding on the nature of the conversation that needs to happen. Ask yourself:

- **What support do I want now?**
- **From whom can I ask for support?**
- **Who else do I want to tell?**
- **What do I want to say?**
- **How and when will I instigate this conversation?**

Keep in mind the basis of relationships that we looked at earlier, using the TRUST model (see page 83):

- **What does it take for me to be TRUE to myself?**
- **How will I ask for RESPECT and show respect to others?**
- **How will I ask for UNDERSTANDING while showing understanding of others and how they may choose to respond to me?**
- **How much SPACE does everyone involved in my life need in order to accept and acknowledge me for who I am?**
- **How much TIME does everyone need in order to accept and acknowledge me for who I am?**

Trust your intuition with these last two questions.

Living life without regret is the key to living your ideal life

Case study: **Jeremy**

Jeremy was nearly 50 and he had been married for 20 years, and had two teenage children. He had known since he was a teenager himself that he was gay. As he grew older, he felt a growing sadness that he was going through the motions of his life, living in a way that society expected, but he knew that he was not being true to himself. He and his wife were good friends and they both loved their children very much. Then one day he met Paul and everything changed. He fell in love for the first time in his life and there was no going back.

Meeting Paul brought reality home to Jeremy. He knew that he needed to take control of his life. The relationship that grew between himself and Paul had to be acknowledged. There was no option to ignore how he felt any more. Following many discussions with Paul, Jeremy knew that the way forward was to be true to himself but in a way that respected those whom he cared about and loved. Jeremy was stunned by the understanding and support he received from his wife and children.

Jeremy and Paul have been together for 10 years now. Jeremy and his wife are still good friends and they meet for supper when they can. Jeremy's children are grown up and they have a very good relationship with both their parents.

Confronting the fear of rejection

Whatever it is that we keep from others about ourselves, whether it is our sexuality, something we believe about ourselves or something in our past, it is fear that holds us back from being truly ourselves. Fear of rejection can control and limit who people choose to be in their lives and hence what they can ultimately achieve.

The price that we pay for not confronting this fear, however, can be to live a life that represents a mere fragment of who we really are. Living life with the same philosophy as coaching encourages people not to stand in judgement of others. If more and more people come to understand the power of coaching in this way, then we will see a significant shift in the world towards greater tolerance and acceptance of differences, along with a celebration of our common humanity.

money

To a child, money represents nothing more than another exciting item to be explored and played with. Yet, by the time we reach adulthood, we have imbued money with all sorts of beliefs and emotions. When couples argue, money is often the number one topic. You may have grown up listening to disagreements between your parents over money, and this may have left you feeling negative about it.

When you are paid a salary that simply appears in your bank account each month, the association with receiving money can be distant. This can change if you ever become self-employed. A negative association with receiving money such as 'I am not deserving' can seriously affect the success of a new venture. Going into business for yourself requires you to put a price on your services and to ask for money in return. This can be challenging if you do not value yourself or what you do.

Money, for some people, is no longer the prime motivator. This does not mean that it has become unnecessary, but simply that people are raising their awareness of what 'enough' means to them, particularly in relation to what they need to do to sustain a certain income level.

Money and your self-esteem

If you are not paid what you feel you are worth for your work, this can generate a sense of not being valued that can lead to feeling low. Maintaining high self-esteem under these circumstances is a challenge that can have a knock-on effect on other

If you do not value yourself, how can you expect anyone else to?

areas of your life. Yet very few people ask for a pay rise. If you do not value yourself, how can you expect anyone else to?

You may even spend money to *try* to make yourself feel better about yourself. Invariably, this has only a short-term benefit. You may have an inner 'spending monster', in the words of Alvin Hall, the financial coach and mentor. Does this monster escape periodically and run amok with your credit cards?

Positive associations

Think about what money can help you to achieve for yourself and others. Having enough money certainly relieves a great deal of the worry that accompanies not having enough. What does 'enough money' mean to you? In what ways do you want money to give you the power to do good in the world?

If you want to create more financial wealth for yourself, then, as you start to coach yourself to achieve this, make sure that your feelings about money are positive and supportive of this goal. Listen to what comes up in the reality section below, in particular, as this is usually where limiting beliefs emerge. If you hear one, revisit the section on how to deal with limiting beliefs (see page 54).

Make sure that your feelings about money are positive and supportive of your goal

USING **TGROW**

TOPIC — Building your future financial security.

GOAL — When you did the wheel of life exercise (see page 60), you may have decided that you want to improve your relationship with money. What needs to happen to achieve this? Remember to focus on expressing what you want in positive terms. Here are a few questions to stimulate your thoughts:

- **What annual income do I want?**
- **How do I want to manage my money?**
- **How much money would I like as savings?**
- **How much money do I want for fun/leisure activities each month?**
- **At what age do I want to be able to stop working if I choose?**
- **When I choose to stop working, what do I want my annual income to be from then on?**

REALITY — **What sort of relationship do I have with money now?**
- **What does money symbolize to me?**
- **In what way does my emotional state influence my financial state?**
- **What level of awareness do I operate with regarding my monthly financial position? For example, do I know approximately how much money I have in my current account right now?**
- **How do I manage my money?**
- **If my source of income was suddenly to disappear, for how long could I support myself?**
- **Do I have all my eggs in one basket?**
- **What is my pension portfolio looking like right now?**
- **How open am I to receiving money?**
- **(If you have a partner) what views do we both have in common regarding money?**
- **Which areas do we disagree on, if any?**

OPTIONS — Depending on the goal that you have chosen regarding money, see how many different ideas you can come up with to move you one step towards that goal.

- How do I see myself managing my money in the future?
- If I knew I could manage money well, what would I be doing differently?
- How many different ways can I think of to generate money?
- What other income-generating activities could I engage in?
- What do I really enjoy doing that I could turn into an income-producing activity?
- If I knew I could do anything, what do I see myself doing that brings money into my life?
- How do I see myself providing an income for my retirement?
- Who do I want to support or to advise me regarding these options?
- Where can I go to understand more about managing money?

WAY FORWARD

– From the list of ideas that you have just generated, decide which one you are most enthusiastic about.

- **What am I actually going to do?**
- **When am I going to start?**
- **What obstacles could get in my way?**
- **How will I overcome these?**
- **How will I measure my progress?**
- **What support do I want?**
- **Who else needs to be involved in or will be affected by what I want to do?**
- **When will I talk to them?**
- **What will I say?**

Consider which other questions you need to ask yourself to have a clear picture of how you are going to move forward now. Check how excited you feel about carrying out the actions that you have planned. If you are not inspired, then revisit your goal and spend time creating one that you *really* want to achieve.

Case study: **Jenny**

Jenny was approaching her 30th birthday. As if that wasn't scary enough, every time she opened a newspaper all she seemed to see were articles about pensions. She was becoming acutely aware that she did not have one and a slight sense of panic had started to creep into her otherwise happy life. One day over a coffee, she mentioned her lack of pension provision to a friend. Sue had recently started paying into a pension and the questions that she had asked herself she now offered to Jenny:

> – **When do I want to be able to stop working?**
>
> – **What do I see myself doing when I don't have to work any more?**

Jenny thought long and hard about what she wanted her life to be like when she was older. She did not find it easy imagining herself when she was 60. However, what she knew that she always wanted to be able to do was to travel, to entertain friends over supper with a bottle of wine and to watch films. So the next questions were simple:

> – **What do I have to do *now* to be able to do this when I am retired?**
>
> – **Who can help me to find out what I need to do?**
>
> – **When will I go and see them?**

The following Saturday saw Jenny discussing her options for a pension with a financial adviser at her bank. She now allocates money every month towards her ideal retirement plan and feels really pleased that she has finally sorted this out.

family

The family you are born into has one of the most important influences on you in your formative years. You adopt the values and beliefs of your parents and those around you as you grow up. You develop your initial sense of identity through your early experiences in this community. In some families, parents want their children to achieve more than they did, and in others the belief is that it is character-building to struggle.

- **How have you been influenced by your family?**

- **What does *family* represent to you?**

- **How satisfied are you with the part of your life that is associated with your family?**

- **If you now have a family of your own, which values and beliefs are you consciously passing on and which ones do you want to discard?**

The importance of listening

Each member of your family is unique. Understanding how to communicate in a way that suits each individual can strengthen the understanding between you. Becoming aware of the different types of listening (see pages 19–22) gives you the opportunity to choose what best suits any interaction you have with a family member, whatever their age. In any family group, differences exist. If you are not sure how to respond to any individual member, the easiest way to find out is to ask them and then *listen* to their response.

Personality types

Consider the mix of personality types you have in your family. Without putting people into categories that can restrict my perception of them, I use four colours to help me respond appropriately to how a person is being at any moment.

Adapted from an idea by Insights Learning & Development Ltd.

COLOUR	PERSONALITY TYPE
RED	Strong-willed, quick-thinking and wanting a quick response because they do not like to waste time. As the colour suggests, these people can also be determined and quite fiery. They can make dynamic leaders.
YELLOW	A 'sunshine' personality, sociable and enthusiastic. They are open, friendly and extrovert. Good people to spend an evening with, sharing stories.
GREEN	Relaxed and amiable, displaying patience and sincerity. They can be encouraging and supportive of others, but risk being taken advantage of because of this. They would make a good chairperson, because they look to include everyone.
BLUE	Cautious and precise, taking time to reflect on decisions. They can be cool and distant, being methodical and task-orientated.

We can all choose to be any colour we want at different times, and also a mixture. You may decide to respond quickly to the needs of a red and not keep them waiting, while respecting that yellows, greens and blues progressively need more time and space to themselves.

- **What colour would best describe who you choose to be most of the time?**
- **What colours best describe the members of your family?**
- **How would you treat these different personalities?**

Family values

A community, however small, operates more successfully when there are commonly agreed values and where all members display mutual respect and understanding. Here are some questions to ask yourself and then explore with each member of your family in turn:

- How truthful do you feel you can be with each other?

- How much respect do you show each other?

- What level of understanding do you show each other?

- How much personal space do you each have or give each other?

- How much family and individual time do you give to each other?

Where there is trust, there is great strength

USING **TGROW**

TOPIC — Your relationship with your family.

GOAL — Imagine that you have your ideal family life. What does it look like to you? Here are some questions to stimulate your thoughts:

- Who do I see?
- What are we all doing?
- What can I hear?
- How do I feel?
- What quality of communication do I want within my family?
- What quality of co-operation do I want within my family?

REALITY — What is the current situation in more detail?
- What roles do I play within my family?
- Which roles do I want to keep?
- Which roles do I want to give up?
- How open to discussing issues are the members of my family?
- What awareness is there of commonly held values?
- What conflicts exist, if any?

– Is there a family member I don't see or speak to any more?
– If there is a disaffected young person in the family, what is going on for me here?
– How do I interact with this young person at the moment?
– If I want advice, which family member would I turn to?
– Who can and does turn to me?
– How much do I feel that each member of the family feels loved and appreciated?
– In what ways does my family show affection and appreciation to me?

OPTIONS
– What options can I come up with to move one step towards the ideal for my family life?
– If I had a magic wand, what transformation would I create?
– If there is a recurring conflict or argument in my family, how can I deal with this differently?
– My own way of seeing or hearing things can be very compelling – in what other ways can I interpret things?
– How can I respond to a disaffected young person differently?
– What changes do I want to see happening?
– What needs to change about *me* to encourage others to consider how they are behaving?

WAY FORWARD
– Which option inspires me most?
– What does this involve me doing?
– Who does this involve me being?
– Who else needs to be involved in this change?
– When and how will I invite them to understand what I want to see happening?
– What conversation needs to happen regarding my role(s) in the family?
– With whom do I need to have this conversation?
– When do I intend to instigate this conversation?
– What am I planning to say?
– How am I planning to say what I want to say in a way that honours and respects my listener(s)?

- How will I measure progress?
- How will we acknowledge each other's contribution and commitment to being a family?
- How will we celebrate our achievements as a family?

Case study: **Christine**

Christine was at her wits' end. There were four in the family, two being teenagers. Mornings were a nightmare – the bathroom had become a battleground. She was not a morning person and her ideal was a quiet, gentle start to the day. The reality was very different – a succession of screaming matches until finally they all managed to leave the house somehow to go to school and work.

Christine decided to create an opportunity to discuss this issue on neutral territory. The following Sunday she suggested that they all go out for lunch for a change. Over lunch, she found a way to introduce the topic of the morning battle for the bathroom. Once she knew that they were really listening to her, she asked her family to understand how she felt about the atmosphere that this created. She explained how she hated the negative energy with which they all left the house and how draining she found it.

Until she voiced how she felt, her family had not appreciated just how much she was being affected by what they saw as normal. Now Paul, her husband, realized he was keen to find a solution. After lots of ideas, one of the teenagers asked if she could have a washbasin in her room so that she could be self-sufficient in the morning. They put washbasins in both their teenagers' rooms, and peace descended.

relationships

This topic includes that one special relationship that you have with a partner or spouse as well as all the relationships that you choose to have with friends, work colleagues and others. We dealt in some detail with relationships on pages 70–76, so you may already have implemented some of the changes that you wanted to make. Remember that change can take time and relapse is normal. Here, the TGROW model is applied to two topics: improving your relationship with your present partner, and finding your ideal partner.

USING **TGROW**

TOPIC – Creating your ideal relationship with your present partner.

GOAL
- **What do I want from an ideal relationship?**
- **What do I see myself doing with my partner?**
- **What do I value in my relationship?**
- **How do I see myself expressing these values?**
- **How do I want to show my partner that I love him/her?**
- **How do I want him/her to show me that he/she loves me?**
- **What are we saying to each other?**
- **What are we doing?**
- **How do I feel?**

REALITY – What is the current situation in more detail?
– What is the quality of the relationship that I have with my partner?
– How much special time do we make for each other?
– How do we show each other that we care?
– Who am I being within this relationship?
– What do I enjoy about this relationship?
– What am I putting up with in this relationship?
– What tends to cause arguments between us?

OPTIONS – What ideas do I have to realize my ideal relationship?
– What needs to change to improve this relationship?
– How can we deal with disagreements differently?
– What do I need to start doing?
– What do I need to stop doing?
– What do I want my partner to start doing?
– What do I want my partner to stop doing?

WAY FORWARD – What am I actually going to do?
– What one action will I take that will move me one step towards my ideal for a relationship?
– When do I intend to take action?
– Who can support me?
– When will I talk to them?
– What other questions do I want to ask myself to complete my understanding of what I am committing to do to achieve my goal here?
– If leaving my partner is what needs to happen, how can I do this without blaming or shaming anyone?

Finding your ideal partner

If the issue is not finding a partner but finding the *right* partner, look again at the case study concerning Rachel (see page 63). After a few months, she felt that her partner was not paying her enough attention. This is what Rachel discovered through coaching:

- **She raised her own awareness of what she wanted from her partner.**
- **She took ownership instead of giving her personal power away.**
- **She realized that he was not telepathic.**
- **She worked out what she wanted to say to him and how she would say it so that he understood what she wanted from him.**
- **She invited him to do the same.**

Attracting your ideal partner requires you to be open to a new relationship coming into your life and being prepared to be pro-active. When you do meet that special someone, remember how valuable the simple TRUST model (see page 83) can be to encourage and support yourself in order to achieve the outcome that you want.

Recall how you got on with the self-esteem questionnaire (see page 96). If you found that your self-esteem needed a boost, assess what you have done so far, and what effect it has had. If you have done nothing, what is holding you back? Coaching works only if you are willing to make changes. If you feel unworthy of a relationship, what needs to happen to change this belief? Revisit the section about changing a limiting belief (see pages 54–57) and work through it to support yourself to succeed.

USING **TGROW**

TOPIC
– Finding your ideal partner.

GOAL
– What am I looking for in a partner?
– What shared values would I like to have with my partner?
– How do I want to be treated?
– What shared interests do I want to have?
– What vision of the future do I have that he/she needs to know about?

REALITY
– What have I done so far to meet my ideal partner?
– What success have I had?
– Where do I go to socialize?
– What do I enjoy doing?
– Where have I been to meet like-minded people?
– When I have met someone, how did I handle the situation?
– What went well?
– What did not go so well? (Remember not to allow your inner critic in here; stay unconditional and non-judgemental)
– What have I learned from my experiences so far?

OPTIONS
– What do I see myself doing differently?
– What new activity would I enjoy becoming involved in where I would meet new people?
– Where can I go that is new and exciting?
– Where do I think I am most likely to meet my ideal partner?
– Who can support me here?
– What can I do to enlarge my network of friends?

WAY FORWARD
– What am I actually going to do?
– Which option really appeals to me?
– When am I going to take action?
– Who do I want to support me?
– What conversation do I need to have, and with whom?
– What am I going to say, and when?
– What other questions do I need to ask myself to become really clear about what I am going to do?

Case study: **David**

David was a single parent. His wife had left nearly 10 years ago when his children were aged seven and five. Since then, he had worked hard to bring them up while working full time. The children were happy and independent, needing less and less of his time and energy now. He began to realize that soon they would be leaving home and he would be on his own. It had been such a long time since he had been in a relationship that he had forgotten what it was like.

David sat down one evening and imagined how his future might be. He saw himself with a partner – someone who shared his interests in music and wine and with whom he could go on holiday. A major obstacle, as David saw it, was that he had not asked a woman out even for a drink in 10 years. His self-esteem where a relationship was concerned was not very high.

After a great deal of thinking, David decided to focus on what he enjoyed doing and to trust that, by beginning to mix more with people outside work, he would eventually meet someone special. He discovered that there was a local wine club that met once a month. He decided to go along and find out more. Not only did he thoroughly enjoy learning about wine with people who shared his interest, but he started to become more comfortable with socializing again. Then Patricia joined the club and David knew that they would become very good friends.

fun and
leisure

We often hear stories these days about people enduring longer and longer working hours and taking fewer holidays, especially in some parts of the developed world. In some other cultures, in contrast, the sharing of a midday meal, followed by a period of rest before work starts again, is sacrosanct. Where we live, and the culture in which we grow up, can have a profound influence on our attitude to the enjoyment of leisure.

Some people are brought up in an atmosphere where relaxing is seen as a 'waste of time' or as being lazy. Do you feel guilty if you are not doing something *useful*? If you measure enjoyment in terms of what has been achieved, then taking time to relax may prove challenging. If you need to spend time justifying what you do, or you live life with a 'time is money' motto, then fun or leisure time may not even be in your repertoire of experiences. These beliefs can also be an important influence on what you decide are your priorities when you are working on the family and relationship sectors of your life. Whatever you hold as your ideal for fun and leisure, you can create what you want.

The work ethic

Burnout from overwork is a very real concept in today's global work culture. In order to live a long and healthy life, considering how you want to balance work and rest is becoming increasingly important. Technological advances have created the ability for rapid communication on a global scale. Instantaneous responses are expected, if not demanded. There is an interdependence between global economies, as well as work patterns that see increased shiftwork creating a consumer demand for round-the-clock service, every day of the year.

It is easy to see how people can be drawn into a 'workaholic' tendency. If a company is not willing to stretch to provide the service that consumers want, then the belief and reality can be that their competitors *will*. Fear of loss alone has the potential to drive the workplace into a frenzy. However, this can also lead to a mentality where it is thought that because you are frantically busy you must be achieving results. This is not always the case.

Taking time out to reflect on issues can produce better results by giving space for more creative thinking. However, taking time out does not mean bringing work home or constantly working late. Finding a clear path that enables you to enjoy work, realize enough money *and* have the quality of life that you want is where coaching comes in.

Work–life balance

Think about what sort of work–leisure balance you want in order for your life to be ideal. Revisiting your core values or what matters to you most in life (see pages 89–94) may be helpful here. It may be that you work so hard that, when you finish work and you have done all the other necessary tasks such as shopping and cleaning, there is no time or energy left to enjoy leisure. It is time to review how you want your life to be with respect to fun and leisure.

> **– What does leisure mean to me?**
>
> **– What does having fun represent to me?**
>
> **– How do I feel if I have nothing to do?**

USING **TGROW**

TOPIC – Making better use of your leisure time.

GOAL – What do I want to enjoy doing when I am not working?
– If I could do anything, what do I see myself doing?
– What have I dreamt of doing that I have never found time for?
– Who am I with?
– Where are we?
– What am I listening to?
– How do I feel?
– How do I relax?
– If I were relaxed, how would I feel?
– What do I see myself doing?

REALITY – What is the present situation in more detail?
– How relaxed do I feel most of the time?
– What do I enjoy doing outside of work at the moment?
– How much time do I have to enjoy myself outside work?
– How much energy do I have left after work to have fun?
– What obstacles can get in the way of me having time out?
– What is holding me back from having more fun?

OPTIONS – What needs to happen for me to enjoy more quality time?
– How do I see myself relaxing on a regular basis?
– What ideas do I have to start enjoying my free time more?
– Who else do I want to spend my leisure time with?
– With what new activities do I want to become involved?
– What needs to happen to overcome any obstacles that can get in the way?

WAY FORWARD – What am I actually going to do?
– What information about new activities do I need to obtain?
– Where will I find this information?
– When will I find time to explore new options?
– Who do I want to support me to improve or increase my leisure time?
– When will I speak to them?
– When do I plan to start enjoying more leisure or fun time?
– How do I intend to measure my progress?

Planning for a successful retirement

Having activities that you enjoy is an important part of planning for a successful retirement. If you only ever work, what will you do when you have more time on your hands later in life? If you are already in retirement and you lack a sense of purpose to each day now that the routine of going to work has gone, then you may find some useful questions in the personal growth section (see pages 118–123).

Case study: **Jane**

Jane was 52, married with two grown-up children. She loved her work but knew that she was also looking forward to a time when she would *not* need to think about the next project and the next set of deadlines. However, Jane was also aware that she had no hobbies as such. When she took a holiday, she preferred to go self-catering, because she got bored easily if she had nothing to do. She had never enjoyed sunbathing and only enjoyed a limited amount of sightseeing. She had begun to ask herself what she was going to enjoy doing when she retired.

Jane decided to explore her natural gifts and talents. She had never seen herself as artistic, because she gave up art in school when she was 12. However, she could sense an artistic or creative streak, because she enjoyed creating a pleasant home environment and inviting friends to dinner. She had recently moved to a house with a pretty garden.

Gardening before was more of a chore than a hobby, but suddenly Jane began to take a real interest in what was growing in the garden and in simple garden maintenance. Jane decided to go to the library and take out a few books on gardening to find out how to look after the plants that she inherited with her new home. She also decided to coach herself consciously on how she planned to enjoy her retirement.

work and
career

The work that we choose to do, and the way in which we choose to do it, can reflect our beliefs about ourselves and work in general. If you do not value yourself or acknowledge your gifts and talents, then you may not apply for a job because you believe that it is beyond you. There are also various myths that many people are brought up to believe, such as 'hard work never hurt anyone', 'if it isn't hard to achieve, it isn't worth achieving' and 'if you want a job doing well, do it yourself'.

It is hardly surprising, therefore, that work-based stress is on the increase, and people are now starting to search for ways to restore a good work–life balance. How many hours you put into your work is less important than what you actually achieve in that time, that is how *effectively* you work. Think about what you can do to *enjoy* the time that you spend at work. If you are working to your strengths, which means doing what you are naturally good at, then work can be a joy rather than a struggle. This is what can influence your quality of life.

Career planning

Career analysts are indicating that, in the world of rapid change that we now live in, young people coming out of school or university can expect to change their careers, not just their jobs, four or five times during their working lives. Around 30 years ago, if you did not stay in a job for more than a couple of years, questions were raised about your loyalty. Nowadays, in constructing a career path, young people are encouraged to move about to gain additional experience and skills that make them more valuable to an employer. Taking a year out to travel can be viewed as an advantage because it displays initiative and can bring a greater understanding of cultural differences.

Today, you need to be aware of, and able to acknowledge, your talents and skills. This requires sound self-esteem. In order to take control of your work career, the future lies in acting like a consultant. Whatever you do, remember that *you* are offering your skills and abilities to an employer who 'buys you in' for a certain period of time, at a certain fee that you negotiate. After that period of time, you seek another contract, and then another. Self-employed people do this all the time. The difference is that, when you sell your labour to an employer, they buy you in at the wholesale price and charge you out at the retail price because they have overheads to deal with. You are not necessarily paid what you are really worth.

When you are self-employed, you may have a little more freedom to choose how hard you work and how much you earn. With fewer permanent employment contracts available now anyway, most people will end up effectively self-employed, which is where a 'portfolio approach' to generating income can reduce the risks associated with a lack of job security.

The portfolio approach

More and more people nowadays talk of a portfolio of income-generating activities. This means that you create more than one opportunity to make money through a range of activities that you enjoy doing. You could have a creative talent, such as painting or photography, that could make a contribution to your overall income without the pressure of having to provide all of it. You might also enjoy teaching a skill or imparting knowledge that you have, in a part-time capacity, that adds to your portfolio. All that is required here is a degree of self-management (see pages 146–147) so that you are not asking too much of yourself.

USING **TGROW**

TOPIC — Making your work or career more fulfilling and enjoyable.

GOAL
- What is your ideal in relation to work?
- If you imagine yourself in your ideal job, what would you be doing?
- What really matters to you in your work?
- What way of working would suit you best?
- What skills or talents do you want to use in your work?
- If you release your true potential, what would you be doing?
- What is your long-term vision for your work?
- What are your boundaries with respect to work?
- How many hours a week do you want to work?
- If you had a portfolio of income-generating activities, what would you be doing?
- Where do you see yourself working?

REALITY
- What makes your work meaningful at the moment?
- What role do you have at work?
- What status do you have at work?
- How appreciated do you feel at work?
- What are you learning about yourself through your work?
- What skills and talents do you use in your work?
- In what ways does your work fulfil you physically, mentally, emotionally and spiritually?
- Where do you work?

OPTIONS
- What ideas do you have for fulfilling your dreams for your work life?
- In what ways could you create your ideal work–life balance?
- What options will enable you to truly enjoy the work that you do?
- If you could work anywhere, where would you be?
- If you cannot do what you love, what could you change in order to love what you do?
- Who can support you?

WAY FORWARD
- From the list of ideas that you have accumulated, which one motivates you to take action?
- What needs to happen now?
- What conversations need to take place and with whom?

- What are you going to say?
- When are you going to start?
- Who do you want to support you?
- Who will be affected by what you want to do?
- When will you discuss your plans with them?
- What obstacles might get in the way?
- How will you overcome these?
- What other questions do you need to ask yourself to be clear about how you plan to move forward now?

Self-management

In order to make sure that you can implement any changes that you decide to make, spend a few minutes checking out your self-management. There is a great deal of talk these days about time management or how to gain an extra hour each day. However, time management is really self-management. When you worked through your physical environment (see pages 112–117), did you decide that you needed to do some organizing and clearing out of clutter? Choosing to take action on clutter will already have had an impact on your self-management, because you may spend less time looking for things.

Some people spend more time planning a two-week summer holiday than they do the rest of their lives. If you apply the 'how long have we got?' principle here, it is almost as if two weeks is how long they have got to really live each year. When you are in a meeting that is about to start, it is good for everyone simply to set the time boundaries for the meeting by asking 'how long have we got?'. Much stress is generated at work because of meetings that overrun, leaving work to pile up that delays your return home.

This can be a useful idea for yourself, too. If you end each day feeling stressed or frustrated that you have unfinished jobs, learning to estimate accurately how many tasks are achievable in one day can be very helpful. Whatever task or activity you are about to do, ask yourself, 'how long have I got?'. Then you can support yourself to stay on track and to achieve what you set out to do each day with ease and a feeling of satisfaction.

Raise your awareness further by answering the following questions:

- How good are you at fitting in everything that you want or need to do each day?

- Do you go through each day calmly moving from one activity to the next?

- How good are you at estimating how long tasks will take you?

- Do you think about or write down a 'to do' list for each day?

- Do you prioritize your activities?

- How good are you at saying 'no'?

Notice that these are closed questions designed to pin you down on your self-management. If you are answering 'no' or 'not very' to most of them, then think about what needs to happen to improve your self-management.

If each day was exactly how you want it to be, what would it be like? Once you have a clear picture of your ideal day, continue to coach yourself on how to achieve it. Here are some questions to stimulate your thoughts:

- What is your average day like at the moment?

- How many things do you try to fit into one day?

- How realistic is this?

- Which activities are priorities?

- How can you work out which activities are essential or non-essential?

- What needs to happen to prevent activities from ending up in the urgent and important category?

- What do you enjoy doing?

- What can you delegate?

- Who can support you?

- What action are you going to take to achieve your goal, and when, where and how will you take it?

Case study: **Charles**

Charles was in his early 30s, married with two small children. He worked as a journalist and had lived in a big city all his life. Now that he had a family, he was beginning to realize how much time and energy he wasted just trying to get to and from work – time and energy he would now rather spend with his wife and children. In addition to this, he and his young daughter had asthma. On the occasions when they left the city and took a holiday by the sea, he noticed that they both breathed more easily. He also realized that he was much more relaxed. Charles decided to adopt a coaching approach to work out how he and his wife Penny could adjust their lives to the benefit of the whole family.

Charles and Penny started by reminding themselves of what really mattered to them in life. They always valued feeling connected and spending time together. The fact that this was happening less and less due to pressures of everyday life was something they had just accepted as normal. However, when they started to look at it consciously, they realized that they had a choice. If this was not how they wanted to live, then what were they going to do about it?

After looking at many options, the one that inspired them both the most was to move to the coast and for Charles to negotiate to work three days in the office and two days from home. If they chose a location that was connected to the city by train, then Charles could commute in less time than it was currently taking him to drive. It took them six months to achieve their goal and Charles knew that taking control of how he chose to work was the best thing he had ever done.

health and
fitness

We are surrounded every day with images of the ideal body. Because of this, many people are living their lives trying to be the clone of a celebrity rather than being true to themselves, and in reality it takes a great deal of time and effort to achieve and maintain the 'perfect' body. It is far better to accept what you can and cannot change. For example, no matter how hard you try, you will never be able to alter your height. So wishing to be taller because of social conditioning is not going to make the slightest difference.

Small is beautiful, big is beautiful – what really matters is how you feel about yourself. Personal happiness comes from within. What is important is acknowledging that you have the power to create your ideal in relation to the body that you were born with and your own personal view of health and well-being.

The mind affects the body and the body affects the mind

Your physical body

It is well acknowledged today that there is a strong connection between mind and body, but how this works is not as yet fully understood. You have already considered how your mind works in terms of self-talk and beliefs (see pages 15–57), so now it is time to think about your body.

How important is it that you feel well and full of energy? If it is not that important, then finding the motivation to make changes may be hard. However, if you are living your life with an 'it won't happen to me' attitude, you may need a wake-up call.

If you can live longer than the previous generation, what do you want to see yourself doing in those extra years – coping with illness longer or enjoying an active life for longer? Thinking ahead like this can help prevent health problems later on. So, ask yourself:

- **How do I treat my body?**
- **In what ways do I take my body for granted?**
- **What habits do I have that could cause my body problems over time?**
- **What do I want to do about these habits?**

Good and bad habits

Many habits are very useful. If you had to *consciously* do everything every day, it would be far more tiring than allowing your body and mind to adopt routines of behaviour that become automatic. Getting out of bed to go to work, cleaning teeth and dressing in the morning are all achieved by many in a semi-conscious state. Once you decide to create a new positive habit, then, if you persevere, after a while what may have felt strange to begin with can soon become normal.

However, there may be some routines that do not serve you or others well. These are habits that can be harmful or irritating, such as smoking, eating too quickly, shouting to get what you want or letting jobs pile up. We have looked at understanding change (see pages 62–67) and found that there is a period where change is contemplated before anything is decided. It is important to allow for relapse, otherwise you can end up giving up at the first hurdle.

Remind yourself of the 'house of change' (see page 102) and how the different components interact. If health and well-being are not high enough on your list of priorities in what matters to you (your core values), then, when life becomes hectic, something like sticking to a certain eating routine can quickly be dropped. This is one reason why resolutions around weight loss and fitness usually do not survive longer than a week or two. It has little to do with willpower and far more to do with priorities, planning and patience (refer back to the case study on page 40, in which Graham changed his attitude to smoking).

Relapse is normal

USING **TGROW**

TOPIC — Creating a new habit, or changing a bad habit, with regard to your health.

GOAL — If I imagine my ideal sense of well-being, what do I see?
— How do I feel?
— What do I see myself doing to maintain this ideal?
— What are people around me saying?
— What is my ideal weight?
— What level of fitness do I have?
— Use SMART (see page 99) to really clarify your goal here.

REALITY — What have I done so far?
— What effect did this have?
— In what ways do my eating habits support me to feel really well?
— What do I choose to do, eat or drink regularly that does *not* help my body to function well?
— When and how do I eat in a way that is not supporting my body well?
— What triggers a bad habit?
— How would I describe my level of fitness at the moment?
— Does this level of fitness enable me to do what I want, such as playing a sport, going for a walk in the hills or gardening?
— What resources do I already have?

OPTIONS — What options can I think of that will move me one step towards my ideal sense of well-being?
— What do I want to start doing to achieve my ideal?
— What do I want to stop doing?
— What obstacles could get in my way?
— How will I overcome these?
— How will I deal with situations that trigger a bad habit?
— Who can support me to achieve my goal here?
— What do I want them to do or to say?

– Which option inspires me most?
– What am I actually committing to doing?
– When will I start?
– What resources do I need?
– How will I measure my progress?
– How will I celebrate each step towards my goal?

Case study: **Stuart**

Stuart was approaching 50 and aware that he had been steadily putting on weight for the past 10 years. Work had demanded more and more of his time, so that he took less and less exercise. He was beginning to feel out of breath when he walked up even a small hill. If he carried on like this, then by the time he was retired, he would be struggling to make the most of his love of the countryside and walking just when he finally had the time to enjoy it.

He was familiar with coaching at work and he decided to apply the same process to his health and well-being. By getting a clear picture of what he saw himself doing when he was retired, he was able to work through what he needed to do now in order to achieve the level of fitness that he wanted. He took an honest assessment of his current fitness and the reality of the time available to him to do something about it. Then he looked at all his options to start to improve the situation. The one that stood out most as the simplest yet most effective was to stop using the lift at work. He worked on the second floor.

Within two weeks, he felt a difference and he has continued to get fitter and trimmer just by using the stairs. The way forward to achieve what you want for your life does not have to be complicated. Often small changes can have a big impact.

The finishing touches

Now that you have coached yourself through the eight segments of your wheel of life, it is time to review your progress and, if necessary, add some finishing touches in order to achieve success in the long term.

Reviewing your progress

Checking your ideal picture

Recall the time you spent at the beginning of this book getting a really clear picture of what you want to create for your life. Bring that picture back into the forefront of your mind now. Think about whether this is still your ideal, or whether in working through the rest of the book you have discovered further changes that you want to make. Identify what else needs to happen, and continue to coach yourself to bring this into reality. Keep going until your life is as you want it to be in every aspect.

Don't settle for second best

Knowing your inner coach

To check how you are getting on with recognizing your inner coach and assess your progress, ask yourself how many of these qualities you can now acknowledge:

- I listen to myself.

- I believe in myself.

- I am non-judgemental and unconditional with myself.

- I encourage and support myself.

- I can challenge myself.

- I keep my focus on what I want to achieve.

- I want the best for myself.

- I acknowledge and celebrate my achievements.

Creating permanent and sustained change

Coaching is a way of being that you can use to enhance every aspect of both the internal life you live with yourself and the external life you share with others at home and at work. Throughout our lives, we have to deal with events, situations and people not of our choosing. However, what we can control is how we choose to respond and deal with these challenges.

If you are tired of your old ways of reacting to situations, use this book to coach yourself through any difficulties and achieve the best possible result. If you make a mistake, you should now have the ability to forgive yourself and move on. Remember, also, that there is nothing wrong with asking for help, if you need it.

Living your ideal life does not require a complete elimination of negative thoughts. The choice is whether you listen and allow your negative inner voice to control you, or whether you choose to believe in yourself *anyway*. In the time that you spend discussing with yourself whether to do something or not, whether you feel like doing it and whether you are capable of doing it, you could actually have done it. There is nothing to stop you adopting a 'just do it' attitude. However, when it comes to goal achievement, there is an interesting reversal of this approach that can be helpful. When you are about to make a decision, ask yourself whether your choice will move you one step towards achieving your goal. If your answer is 'no', then in this case the situation might actually benefit from a 'don't do it' option. Use your inner coach to help you make the right decision.

Life design

I trust that you feel you have a clearer understanding of what matters to you in life, what has held you back in the past and what your intentions are for your life now and in the future. Remember, you are the architect of your own life.

Taking responsibility

Coaching helps to raise your awareness and encourages you to take responsibility for your life, acknowledging your resourcefulness and trust that you can face the unknown. When you know that, whatever happens in your life – the unexpected, the unknown – you can deal with it; once you are comfortable and secure in who you are, then you are 'in play' with the game of life. You will think about, not what you can take from the world, but what you can bring to it – *you*. You are more than enough. You bring your uniqueness, your imagination, your curiosity, your creativity and your love.

When you can say 'I am resourceful' and 'I can trust myself', then you will be able to handle any situation by considering what needs to happen, how you will achieve it, and whose help you might need. Continue to supply and face your own information unconditionally and without self-judgement.

Anything is possible

Whatever it is that you want to create in your life, remember that, if it is possible for others, then it is possible for you. If you really want to do something, you will find a way. Coaching helps you to:

- **keep looking for a way of seeing things that uplifts you**
- **look for questions that challenge your thinking**
- **continue to listen for the brilliance inside you**
- **never give up on yourself**
- **there is no right way to live your life, there is only your way that works.**

Making a difference

After living your ideal life, think about what you will want to reflect back on. Your contribution may be to raise a family and to pass on wisdom that will help to sustain the world. You may have been a joy to work with or to live with, someone who brought a smile to another person's face.

By now, I hope that you can recognize that if your work feels *heavy* and you have to drag yourself through each day to do it, then maybe this is not your true work – coach yourself and find out. If your 'work' seems to flow and be almost effortless, this can be one sign that you are working at making a difference. Look for other signs that can indicate to you whether or not you are doing what you were really meant to do.

If you take your life in phases, what you do when you are 25 may be different to what you do when you are 55. If you choose, or have chosen, to have children, when they have left home you can decide what to do with all that creative energy. One theme that can run throughout your life is what you value. If you are true to your core values, there are many ways in which you can choose to express them.

Whatever you contemplate for yourself in the future, always involve your inner coach, who can guide you to success.

Recipe for SUCCESS

to **SUCCEED**:

S ORT OUT YOUR CORE VALUES

U NDERSTAND THE IMPACT OF YOUR BELIEFS ON WHAT YOU ACHIEVE IN LIFE

C HOOSE **SMART** GOALS

C HECK THEIR ALIGNMENT WITH YOUR VALUES AND BELIEFS

E NJOY **GROW**ING WITH YOUR INNER COACH

E VALUATE YOUR PROGRESS AND **TRUST** YOURSELF TO:

D ESIGN YOUR IDEAL LIFE.

Have a great life!

Bibliography
and further reading

Berman Fortgang, Laura, *Take Yourself to the Top* (London: HarperCollins, 1998)

Butler, Gillian, and Tony Hope, *Manage Your Mind* (Oxford: Oxford University Press, 1995)

Carr, Allen, *Easy Way to Stop Smoking* (London: Penguin, 1999)

Covey, Stephen, *Seven Habits of Highly Effective Families* (New York: St Martin's Press, 1998)

Downey, Myles, *Effective Coaching* (London: Orion, 1999)

Edwards, Gill, *Pure Bliss* (London: Piatkus, 1999)

Foster, Helen, *Dejunk Your Life* (London: Aurum Press, 2002)

Goleman, Daniel, *Emotional Intelligence* (London: Bloomsbury, 1996)

Grant, Anthony, and Jane Greene, *Coach Yourself* (London: Pearson Education, 2002)

Hall, Alvin, *Money For Life* (London: Hodder & Stoughton, 2000)

Harris, Gina, *Life Coaching – Connecting You to Your Inner Wisdom* (Chichester: Kingsham Press, 2002)

Harris, Thomas, *I'm OK – You're OK* (London: Arrow Books, 1995)

Kingston, Karen, *Creating Sacred Space with Feng Shui* (London: Piatkus, 1996)

Kline, Nancy, *Time to Think* (London: Cassell, 1999)

Jampolsky, Gerald, *Love is Letting Go of Fear* (Berkeley, CA: Celestial Arts, 1979)

Jeffers, Susan, *End the Struggle and Dance with Life* (London: Hodder & Stoughton, 1996)

Lindenfield, Gael, *The Positive Woman* (London: HarperCollins, 1992)

Neenan, Michael, and Windy Dryden, *Life Coaching – a Cognitive-Behavioural Approach* (Hove: Brunner-Routledge, 2002)

Orman, Suze, *The Courage To Be Rich* (London: Vermilion, 1999)

Richardson, Cheryl, *Take Time For Your Life* (London: Bantam Press, 2000)

Richardson, Cheryl, *Stand Up For Your Life* (London: Bantam Press, 2002)

Smith, Hyrum, *What Matters Most* (London: Simon & Schuster UK, 2000)

Stewart, William, *Building Self Esteem* (Oxford: How To Books, 1998)

Whitmore, John, *Coaching for Performance* (London: Nicholas Brealey Publishing, 3rd edition, 2002)

Whitworth, Laura, Henry Kimsey-House, Phil Sandahl, *Co-Active Coaching* (Palo Alto, CA: Davies-Black Publishing, 1998)

Williams, Nick, *The Work We Were Born To Do* (Shaftesbury: Element Books Ltd, 1999)

Zohar, Danah, and Ian Marshall, *Spiritual Intelligence – the Ultimate Intelligence* (London: Bloomsbury Publishing, 2001)

Index

Acknowledgements

Author's Acknowledgements:

This book would not exist without the constant love, support and encouragement that I receive from my husband, John. His belief in my ability to achieve has kept me going and the result is witnessed on every page in this book. My thanks also go to my grown-up children, Carolyn and Edward, whose support has been uplifting and who are an endless source of joy in my life. I am grateful to my sister, Carrie Johnson for her wisdom and feedback. Peter Barclay, with whom it is a constant pleasure to work, has given me valued encouragement throughout this project. I would like to thank all the Coaches at the UK College of Life Coaching for their friendship and the opportunity to explore and deepen our understanding of coaching together. They are a special group of people who are committed to assisting other people to achieve. My thanks also go to Trevor Davies and Alice Tyler, my editors for their guidance and support in developing this book.

Pam Richardson, Principal of the UK College of Life Coaching; www.ukclc.net

Publisher's Acknowledgements:

Executive editor: **Trevor Davies**
Editor: **Leanne Bryan**
Executive art editor: **Leigh Jones**
Design: **Ruth Hope**
Illustration: **David Beswick**
Senior production controller: **Martin Croshaw**